Observing Young Children

D0144136

This fully revised second edition of *Observing, Assessing and Planning for Children in the Early Years* provides a detailed analysis of what is meant by the observation of young learners and why this is so vital to early years practitioners and students. In this accessible and insightful text, Sandra Smidt examines the various theories of how young children develop and learn, which have been put forward by thinkers and writers across time and place so that the reader has a genuinely global view of early childhood. She then highlights how important it is for practitioners in schools, nurseries and settings to think carefully about what they have seen and heard in light of what they, as adults, already know about the children and their learning.

Also included in this text are helpful 'Try your hand' sections where readers are invited to make their own judgements about what they have read, as well as a section on observing and assessing not only nursery-aged children but also babies and toddlers.

Sandra Smidt is a writer and consultant in early years education. She has previously written *The Developing Child in the 21st Century, 2nd edition* (2013), *Introducing Malaguzzi* (2012), *Introducing Bruner* (2011), *Playing to Learn* (2010) and *Introducing Vygotsky* (2008), all published by Routledge.

Essential Guides for Early Years Practitioners

Observing Young Children

The role of observation and assessment in early childhood settings

Second edition

Sandra Smidt

Routledge
Taylor & Francis Group

LONDON AND NEW YORK

KH

Second edition published 2015
by Routledge
2 Park Square, Milton Park, Abingdon, Oxon OX14 4RN

and by Routledge
711 Third Avenue, New York, NY 10017

Routledge is an imprint of the Taylor & Francis Group, an informa business

© 2015 Sandra Smidt

First edition published 2005 by Routledge as *Observing, Assessing and Planning
for Children in the Early Years*

British Library Cataloguing-in-Publication Data
A catalogue record for this book is available from the British Library

Library of Congress Cataloging in Publication Data
Smidt, Sandra, 1943–
    [Observing, assessing, and planning for children in the early years]
    Observing young children : the role of observation and assessment in
    early childhood settings / Sandra Smidt. — Second edition.
        pages cm. — (Essential guides for early years practitioners)
    Revised edition of: Observing, assessing, and planning for children
    in the early years.
    Includes bibliographical references and index.
    1. Observation (Educational method) 2. Early childhood education.
    I. Title.
    LB1027.28.S65 2014
    372.21—dc23
    2014038522

ISBN: 978-1-138-82355-6 (hbk)
ISBN: 978-1-138-82356-3 (pbk)
ISBN: 978-1-315-74198-7 (ebk)

Typeset in Perpetua and Bell Gothic
by Florence Production Ltd, Stoodleigh, Devon, UK

Printed and bound in the United States of America by Publishers Graphics,
LLC on sustainably sourced paper.

5/9/16

The first edition of this book was dedicated to my grandchildren Hannah, Ben, Chloe, Jacob and Zac in recognition of all the significant moments they revealed to me in their early years. Their early years are over but they continue to reveal significant moments as they continue to think and question, take chances and try new things. No longer early learners, they are — like us all — lifelong learners.

Contents

Acknowledgements

My thanks to both Mary Jane Drummond and Birgit Voss for permission to reproduce both their work which originally appeared in both editions of *The Early Years: A Reader* (first edition) / *Key Issues in Early Years Education* (second edition), which I edited.

Preface

This is the second edition of a book I wrote in 2005 as part of a series of books published by Nursery World and Routledge. It was called *Observing, Assessing and Planning for Children in the Early Years*. In the decade or so since then my thinking has developed and the world has changed. Ten years is a long time both in publication and in education. Some things remain unchanged: young children are always curious and questioning from the moment they are born, and possibly before that; the adults around them support them in their attempts to make sense of their world and the children learn from everything that happens to them and all their encounters with others in this social world of ours. But other things do change and one of these is thinking about teaching and learning. As a young child you might have felt you had to be quiet around adults. Nowadays it is likely that you encounter young children who are made to feel that they are the centre of the universe. Patterns of thinking about children and childhood and education change over time, often as governments – with their particular ethos and philosophy – change. Since the education of young children is a matter for society the expectations of what young children should and should not do change, inevitably, together with the ways in which those caring for and educating them think or are told to think.

This book carries the same title as the first edition but has been almost completely revised in response to critiques of the first book made by serious and respected experts and my own determination that this should not be a 'how to' book but a serious examination of what is meant by assessment, how good assessment sits neatly with good teaching and learning and how what we assess needs to fit into a model where the child is seen as a competent and questioning meaning maker in communities of other competent meaning makers. It has little or nothing to do with tick boxes, targets or goals.

The book is set out in a particular way in order to enable you to attempt to find your own answers to some of the questions asked and the issues raised. So in each chapter there is a section headed 'Try your hand' where you are invited to make decisions about what you have read. Being able to make a decision, a choice, an evaluation or a judgement is an essential part of being a good assessor and a good practitioner. This book, about observation, assessment and planning, is about the very processes of looking and listening carefully; making a record of what is seen and heard; using that record to evaluate what you have seen and heard against what you know and also for planning ahead. Sometimes you are given an answer and sometimes not.

Chapter 1

The questioning child

My mother says parents make their own children. How can people make people – all by themselves?

Five-year-old Jill asks this question during a discussion of where babies come from in the classroom of Vivian Gussin Paley (1981: 75). Like all children Jill is seeking to make sense of her world and verbally making clear just what it is she wants to know.

This chapter is called 'The questioning child' for a reason. In many educational settings children are required to *answer* questions. Relatively little attention is paid to children asking questions despite the fact that many researchers, writers and theorists have noted that young children are constantly raising questions as they make sense of their worlds. The reasons for this include the possibility – indeed the likelihood – that 'asking' a question implies the use of spoken language and many of the questions children raise are not verbal but have to be deduced from watching what the children do and listening to what they say.

In this, the opening chapter of this book, we examine what is currently thought about how children learn and develop in order that our understanding of what we see and hear is an *informed understanding*.

CHILD DEVELOPMENT

A common sense definition of child development might be that it is a discipline (or an area of study) which examines how the human infant develops from dependence to independence, in terms of physical, social, emotional and cognitive growth and change. It is a broad discipline encompassing a range of views, the majority of which focus on the development of children in the developed world rather than those in the developing world. This is a serious issue because it carries implications in terms of what is *not* addressed. Since one of the aims of this book is to help you to recognise good practice and become an advocate for it you need to become aware and critical of what you read.

We know that children throughout the world learn to do complex things. Babies learn to smile at familiar faces; look intently at something they desire; move to the rhythms of music; grasp and hold and then manipulate objects; sit and creep or crawl and then walk and hop and run and jump. They learn to communicate through pointing and eye pointing, intonation, gesture and language. They become able to express their thoughts and feelings in myriad ways. And all of this without a single formal lesson.

Let's look at some of the key figures in early childhood development and summarise what they said in terms of helping us understand what they were saying. The theorists have been selected in terms of both their influence on thinking but also because they share my view that child development must take account of the essential issues of where and with whom the child is learning and developing. My view is a sociocultural one, a view that I hope you will share if not now then when you have read this book. We will return to some of these theorists together with some additional writers in the next chapter when we think about the adults and their role in child development.

Jean Piaget was a Swiss biologist who studied his own children individually and local children in groups. He was interested in cognitive (or intellectual) development and was the first person to notice that children are not passively acted on by the world but actively make meaning, initially through their senses and movement. Before this it had been believed that the infant was a blank slate waiting to be written on by experience. Piaget saw the *child as an active learner*. He saw learning as progressing through *age-related stages* with the learner only being able to move on once she was ready for the next stage. This model has a focus on what the child *cannot yet do* and this applies also to his notion that young children are *egocentric* and cannot take on the perspective of others. As we will see, this has been firmly disputed. He was, however, interested in *play* (or self-selected activity) *and its role in learning* and his thinking on how and why children often engage in repeated patterns of action (or *schemas*) is often useful in understanding observed behaviour. If you are interested in his very significant ideas and contribution read *Introducing Piaget* by Ann Marie Halpenny and Jan Pettersen (2014).

Lev Vygotsky was a Russian psychologist, who died young and whose work was not published in the UK until the 1960s. He was interested in how knowledge is passed on from generation to generation, which meant he was deeply *concerned with culture*. He said that children come to understand their world through their *interactions with more experienced others* and through the *use of cultural tools* – by which he meant language, art, music, symbols and signs, all of which are developed by groups in society. He shared with Piaget the view of children as active learners, but – by believing that learning takes place through the interactions learners have with others – his view is much more social.

He also shared with Piaget an interest in play as a mode of learning and famously said that observing a child at play allows us to see the child 'standing a head taller than himself'. He placed tremendous emphasis on language and how children acquire or learn their first *language(s)*, taking account of *the role of others, of mediation and memory and internalisation*.

To learn more about his very significant ideas and contribution read *Introducing Vygotsky* by Sandra Smidt (2008).

Jerome Bruner was born in the United States and born blind. He was initially concerned with two issues: why so many young children fail in formal education in the UK and the interactions infants have with their primary caregivers (usually mothers) in the rituals or *formats* (things like the Peekaboo games) of early childhood. He saw this as being the start of *intersubjectivity* where the child becomes social. Like Vygotsky he believed it was essential to take note of *culture and context* which he saw as being essential to learning and development. He, too, was very interested in *play as a mode of learning*, including the playing of games and wrote a great deal about *language*, focusing on many aspects, but latterly and most importantly on the *significance of narrative* or story making/story telling. For him this was the way in which young children not only made sense of their experiences but were able to order and share these so as to better understand them.

To learn more about his very significant ideas and contribution read *Introducing Bruner* by Sandra Smidt (2011).

Loris Malaguzzi was born and educated in the wealthy region of Emilia Romagna. Based at Bologna University after the war he became committed to the idea of providing early childhood education for children that was not run by the church. He was instrumental in helping peasant women in the Reggio Emilia region of Italy set up a series of nursery schools to provide educational opportunities for very young children. Underpinning his work was an ideology based on the notion of *each child*

3

being both unique and competent and of every child having access to what he called 'a hundred languages' — by which he meant the resources (or what Vygotsky called the *cultural tools*) to allow them to express their thoughts and feelings and theories in as many different ways as possible. Not surprisingly he was concerned by injustice, the impact of poverty and oppression, the significance of culture and class and family. He noticed that *children's questions (spoken or implied) show what they are thinking* — what he called their *theories* — and that these could be used to take learning to very complex levels.

To learn more about his very significant ideas and contribution read *Introducing Malaguzzi* by Sandra Smidt (2012) or books by Carlina Rinaldi or Via Vecchi.

TRY YOUR HAND

Throughout this book you will come across sections like this where you are invited to have a go at being an active learner yourself by applying what you have just read to the given task.

When I was a small child we lived in a seaside town in South Africa. One day, on a visit to the docks I came across a structure I had not before noticed. It was made of something very hard, painted black, a little taller than I was and shaped with something like a head and a body. I explored it thoroughly and then announced to my parents, 'I seed it and I feeled it and it is not a dog.'

What do you think Piaget, Vygotsky, Bruner or Malaguzzi would have said about my development? Think about my actions and my words, remembering that I was only 3 years old at the time. (Note: please see page 9 for my analysis.)

Many people are critical of the fact that the most famous and influential theorists adopt a monocultural view of child development. Some talk of *everybaby* which implies that one baby is pretty much like another when, in reality, you must know that the world is made up of babies of different genders, from different backgrounds, learning different languages, but all learning and developing.

Barbara Rogoff is an American researcher, deeply interested in the importance of groups and culture, who looks at children in the developing world and sees how they learn through being active participants in the real-life events of their communities. She talks of these learners as 'apprentices' saying that the learning happening can be described as and called '*guided* *participation*'. Replicating meaningful contexts or events similar to the everyday activities and events in the home in the classroom or setting may lead to building a classroom/setting culture of shared values, shared cultural tools and shared expectations. Think about how meaningful contexts, where the purpose of activities is clear to the children, will make what Margaret Donaldson called *human sense* to them.

Urie Bronfenbrenner, an ecologist, was concerned with describing the network of contexts available to all children. In his model, the child is at the centre and around the child is a microsystem made up of the home in which are the child, parents and, possibly, siblings and extended family members; the religious setting in which are the child, peers and adults; the school or setting, in which are the child, educators and peers; and the neighbourhood, in which are the child, adults and peers. The first of the concentric circle describes the mesosystem, which defines the interactions between home, school, neighbourhood and religious settings. Next is the exosystem, describing the impact (real or potential) of such things as local industry, parents' workplaces, local government, mass media and the school or setting management committee. Finally, and most remote from the child, are the macrosystems, which define the dominant beliefs and ideologies operating for that child and his or her family. Into this come things such as laws. This model firmly *situates every child in the cultural layers*, close and remote, which will impact on her development.

Throughout the world there are millions of children who grow up knowing more than one language. There are *many cognitive advantages to being bilingual* and these include a greater awareness of how language itself operates, which can help with the development of literacy, enhance problem-solving skills and build recognition of the importance of both context and audience. There are many people who have worked in this field including **Jim Cummins**, **Colin Baker**, **Eve Gregory** and **Charmian Kenner**. All of this reminds us that context and culture must always inform our thinking about development.

Judy Dunn's research focused on very young children and how they came to *make sense of the rituals, rules and conventions relating to social interaction*. Her study involved her examining interactions in families and, although it was situated within one smallish community or context, it has relevance more widely. Most interestingly, she showed how early in life children develop an understanding that others have feelings and needs. It laid the foundation for later work on *intersubjectivity* and firmly challenged Piaget's notion of young childrens' inability to *decentre*.

Colwyn Trevarthen found that infants as young as 2 months of age show a different response to someone who speaks to them than to someone else in the room who remains silent. In his studies of babies together with their primary caregivers he was able to document the ongoing interchange between the two. Through this *the infant begins to understand the feelings and intentions of the adult.*

Carlina Rinaldi, who worked very closely with Malaguzzi, tells us that, from birth, the infant is engaged in building a relationship with the world and intent on experiencing it so that she develops a complex system of abilities, strategies for learning and ways of organising relationships. So she is able to make her own *personal maps* for her own development and orientation – maps which are social, cognitive, emotional and symbolic.

Gopnik, **Meltzoff** and **Repacholi** propose that development proceeds by *a constant process of revision as the child makes sense of her interactions with others. So the child starts out with some assumptions and then tries out* her theories and evaluates them and tries again. The child cobbles together her understanding as she interacts with others.

Twardosz (2012), a neuroscientist, talks of experience-dependent plasticity which involves the modification of existing synapses or connections in the brain or the generation of new ones on the basis of individually specific experience. This is what *enables individuals to become members of their own culture.* So a child in Hanoi might eat using chop sticks, whilst a child in a village in the Sudan might eat with her fingers; Spanish children learn to read text from left to right, whilst children learning Arabic learn to read from right to left. You can see from these examples how learning and memory work. Any child is born into a context of a community, a society, a set of values and customs and beliefs and traditions. The child experiences what exists within her culture. The connections in her brain are affected by what she sees and does. This experience-dependent plasticity occurs throughout life and there are no sensitive or critical periods. In summary this says that we learn through all our experiences, wherever and whenever they take place.

Bame Nsamenang is associate professor of psychology and learning science at the University of Bamenda, Cameroon and founding director of the Human Development Resource Centre, a research and service facility for research into human development. Nsamenang says that much of current thinking about child development in Africa focuses on the child as being very much the *agent of her own learning and development.* In many African cultures parents do not consciously raise their children in the sense of getting them ready for each successive stage of a formal education process (as so many do in the West), but create participative spaces where the children emerge and mature by themselves out of one set of developmental tasks into another. This is very similar to some of the examples from South America given by Rogoff, such as the small child who sits and watches older children involved in making tortillas. At first she just watches. Then, perhaps, she is given a lump of dough to play with. Later still she is given one or two necessary tools. Eventually she is a full participant in the tortilla making process. It is a process from being co-participants in real life activities first as novices within peer groups and later as recognised, respected and full participants in the life of the family and community.

This is a lot of information to come to terms with so here is a summary of the key findings for you to be aware of. You will know much of this but being reminded can be helpful.

IN SUMMARY

What we learn from the research and ideas of others about how young children develop and learn:

- Children's learning takes place always within social, cultural and linguistic contexts. So relationships with other people, children and adults, matter. They learn at home, in their neighbourhoods, in the playground, in virtual worlds. They learn from what they see and hear and this may be in one or more languages. All languages equip children equally with the means to communicate. Their earliest learning is rooted in daily life where they have access to real events whose purpose is clear and where they are inducted into the rules and rituals and conventions of their homes. As they move away from the security of this they become more and more able to deal with the abstract. You need to know as much as possible about the children in your care to understand what they are interested in or paying attention to or raising questions about.
- Children are born both curious and competent in the sense that they actively make meaning and share meaning with others. They are not waiting to be filled with knowledge but engage with everything that happens to them, trying to understand it all. To do this they raise questions which they ask or imply through their actions and responses.

- Children use whatever is available in terms of languages and tools, physical and cultural, to both find answers to their questions and express their feelings.
- Behaviours that appear to be random and senseless can be understood in terms of trying to establish what it is the child is trying to make sense of.
- Children learn through their interactions with others – adults and children. Where they are able to share attention with others they can get deeply engrossed in what they are interested in. Anybody who says that young children have a limited concentration span has clearly not paid careful attention to them. Play – which is where children can follow their own interests and passions – is a primary mode or way of learning precisely because a child who is able to raise a question that matters to her will be very interested in finding an answer. So play is a serious business.
- Children establish strong and important relationships from birth and much of their learning in the earliest years comes about through the games or formats that are played in the home, the daily routines and rituals, the sounds of their home languages and the enacting of rules, roles and conventions in meaningful contexts.
- Words like agency and ownership are important when thinking about children's development. They are, of course, linked to being an active learner. Where a child, fascinated or puzzled by something, tries to find out about it she takes ownership of the problem she has set herself. When we, the adults, allow the child to continue with her meaning search we are allowing her agency over her own learning. Sadly, in many settings, what children learn is determined by others rather than the child herself. In developing countries adults more willingly allow children to retain agency.
- As meaning makers children structure their experiences, sequencing events and organising them, in order to make sense of what has happened. This requires them engaging in higher order cognitive processes of thought, including memory, comparison, and reasoning. It is the beginning of narrative. The earliest little protonarratives do not need a conventional beginning, middle and end, but merely the logical connection of two or more events. Here is Octavia's protonarrative, told when she was 4 years old:

> *Once upon a time when I was little in my garden there were an earthworm coming out of my plant.*

Holding a view of the child as a competent, curious, communicative and feeling being will help you keep your focus on what the child knows and can do.

MY RESPONSE TO THE QUESTION ASKED IN THE 'TRY YOUR HAND' SECTION IS THIS:

Piaget would possibly have commented on my grammatically incorrect use of the past tense but praised the fact that I explored the unfamiliar object using my senses and movement, which he would have regarded as appropriate to my age, whilst Bruner might have liked the fact that I turned the experience into a simple narrative with a beginning, a middle and an end. This allowed me to recall, order and share my experience with my parents. Vygotsky would have applauded my ability to analyse what I had done to answer the question I had set myself – 'What is this thing?' – and noted that I was able to remember past experiences and make comparisons with what I already knew. Both of these are higher order thinking skills. Malaguzzi would probably have invited me to explore it further using some of my hundred languages like drawing, painting and making.

MOVING ON

In this opening chapter we have looked at some of those who have contributed to our understanding of how young children develop and learn. Knowing something about this is essential to being able to make sense of what children say and do as active learners. It is the beginning of a foundation on which to build.

Chapter 2

The informed adult

This makes them unhappy . . . They cannot see. They cannot hear. They cannot breathe . . . Dibs, dig them out of there.

(Axline 1964: 67)

In 1964 a respected play therapist called Virginia Axline wrote a book called *Dibs in Search of Self* where she traced the progress of a 5-year-old boy called Dibs, who had been described by his school as being a 'defective'. Through her observations of Dibs at play Axline began to understand his fears, his dreams and his abilities. She was not a teacher but a play therapist, trained in the skills of close observation as the primary tool to understanding behaviours which seemed strange or unacceptable. In her book Axline described just how, through her observations of Dibs, she was able to understand the issues that frightened him and caused him to be such an anxious child. In one of her sessions with him he identified one of the soldiers as 'Papa' and proceeded to knock him down time and time again.

Those of us working with young children in schools and settings are not primarily concerned with treating children but rather with understanding what they can do, what they are interested in and what they already know. I would suggest that few of us have had any in-depth training into what the process of observation as an educational tool involves.

BECOMING A THINKING ADULT

You may have heard of **Susan Isaacs** who started an experimental school called the Malting House School in Cambridge. Over a 3-year period from 1924 to 1927 she kept detailed observation notes of the children at play. Her purpose was to throw light upon both the intellectual and the social development of these children. Her initial aim had been to write about both aspects in one book, but the material gathered revealed so much that she produced one whole volume focusing solely on intellectual development – the now famous but out of print *Intellectual Growth in Young Children*. If you are fortunate enough to read this book I am sure you will discover, as I did, that she often finds it impossible to focus solely on the intellectual since, as you will know, all learning involves the social, the cultural and more. As she had a great interest in psychology many of her observations were analysed in terms of her thinking about the child's emotional well-being.

Let us take Isaacs as a model of how to become a thinking practitioner. Unlike Axline she did not have the luxury of being able to focus on one child at a time. Rather she was working with groups and she insisted that there should be nothing of the sense of the children being tested in any way. She set out to watch and listen to the children in order to understand each child as a whole being – one who laughs and cries, plays and argues, thinks and asks questions. Here is the crucial link with the first chapter in this book. Isaacs understood that children at play with others or alone are often engaged in answering a question they themselves have raised. So she was looking at a group of largely privileged children, some of whom were boarding at the school, interested primarily in what they said as they played. The focus of her book is on spoken language – what the children said aloud to themselves or to others as they experimented and played – and what is revealed through analysing that.

For many of you working in classrooms, playgroups, daycare centres or other settings, observing children is what you do. You do it in the garden or playground, when the children work and play, when they arrive and leave, at lunch and snack times. You do it in much the same way as we watch and listen to people when we sit in a café or a bus or a park bench. We take notice of what we see and hear and it sometimes entertains and amuses us and gives us things to comment on or talk about. You will be able to remember some of the funny things you have heard children say during the day and then commented on these to your colleagues or others. More recently some childcare workers have been trained to observe children closely and do this as part of their everyday work. In order for observation to become a useful tool to you in terms of understanding the children you work with and planning for their learning and development, the whole process needs to become more conscious and more organised. You will need to think about the place of observation in the whole cycle of children's learning and development.

TRY YOUR HAND

Mary Jane Drummond (1998) cites the story of a 4-year-old girl looking at a collection of shells, rocks and pebbles, using an assortment of magnifiers of different sizes and shapes.

The child spends a considerable amount of time moving from one object to another, one magnifier to another. She eventually puts a shell that she finds most interesting under the tripod of the magnifying glass. She looks at the shell, moving her head up and down until she seems satisfied. Then she picks it up and holds it to each ear in turn. Then she puts it back on the table, again under the magnifying lens and places her ear close to the lens as if she were listening to it through the magnifying glass.

Read this again and say what you think the child is doing. Do you think this is random behaviour? Is the child foolish for thinking a magnifying glass would affect sound? Read Mary Jane's analysis of this and see if you agree with it. We will return to Drummond's ideas in the last chapter of this book.

As I watched I realised she was asking a question, not out loud, but privately, to herself. She had established that the magnifying glass made the shell look bigger, now she wanted to know 'will it make it louder?'

(1998: 38)

Here is another child for you to think about.

Ozman is 5 and he seems really interested in things that spin. He draws circles and wheels, twirls round and round in the playground, spins things in the air. He will spend hours spinning tops, tracking their paths and comparing one with another. Sometimes this play is totally engrossing and he is silent, but sometimes he talks himself through it, making a running commentary about what he is thinking.

A thinking observer will begin to notice that the toys are just a vehicle for his interest in things that spin: in rotation itself. The thinking observer could only come to this conclusion through watching Ozman on different occasions, doing different things. Noticing Ozman's preoccupation with rotation you might have made the link to Piaget's work on schemas.

Having noticed and analysed something about an individual child you have the starting point for planning activities that will build on what the child has demonstrated an interest in. Your careful observation is key to planning for learning.

Carlina Rinaldi tells us that *listening* is the premise for any kind of learning relationship. You certainly listen to the children you work with but could you certainly say that you listen attentively, with a real concern to find out what it is that the child wants you to hear? The essence of listening in learning is that it is reciprocal, often initiated by the child because the child has a question, an interest, a theory or a passion and she is turning to you to invite you to share that. Parents are often better at doing this than teachers and other practitioners, partly because they have such a strong relationship with the child and are almost inevitably interested in what the child is saying. When my daughter Sam was a very little girl she said, 'We are oppositing each other, aren't we?' and I was stunned at her inventiveness and replied, 'What a wonderful word. Yes. We are sitting opposite each other and you have invented a new word – oppositing. It's wonderful. It says everything in one word. You are clever.' Easy for me because there were no other children requiring my attention at that moment, no learning goals or targets to tick, just the delight of the interaction.

One of the most important things we can learn from Malaguzzi's ideas and those of his successors like Rinaldi is the importance of this kind of listening in educational settings. They call it *active listening* – a phrase that really pleases me because it gives the clear sense of it taking place between equal partners and thus reciprocal. The child has an idea or a question or a theory and she tells it to you. You listen and in this way she allows you to glimpse what is taking place in her mind. She implicitly invites you to respond in some way. Your response allows her to confirm or change her idea. It is a wonderful communicative verbal dance.

TRY YOUR HAND

This time you are being invited to examine what the adult in the example below does and evaluate it in terms of its potential effect on the children and their learning. Being conscious of what other adults around you do and say is important and becoming evaluative about that can be a powerful learning tool for you.

A group of 4-year-olds in Honolulu were outside playing when a gust of wind blew across the yard. 'That's the windy wind,' one child said. The teacher asked, 'The windy wind. Are there different kinds of wind?' Soon a gentle breeze wafted across their faces and another child said, 'There, that was a gentle wind.'

(Forman and Fyfe 2012, in Edwards *et al. 2012: 260*)

It is relatively easy to identify what the adult did in this example. She took notice of something the child said, thought about what it revealed about the child's thinking and asked a question in return. This not only let the child know that she had been listened to seriously but implicitly invited the other children in the group to join in the dialogue. The fact that the child had not asked a question requiring an answer but had described the wind as the windy wind was evidence that she had a theory which was that there may be different kinds of wind in that place. It takes great skill, sensitivity and practice to be able to do this but it is certainly something you can learn to do.

The importance of this example is that it shows how being genuinely interested in what the children say and do enables the children to allow you into their minds. They admit you by the questions they ask, the actions they take and the things they say. One of the key features of your role as educator is to be alert and sensitive to all you see and hear. As you listen and observe, you need to draw on what you know both about the individual children involved but also about aspects of child development. This active listening is one of the most important ways in which children can be helped to think and question, develop their own hypotheses or theories, express these in some way to the adults who then respond in a way that helps the child's thinking and learning move on. It is important to remember and keep reminding yourself that questions need not be explicit; they need not be verbal. What children say or do offers clues to what they are seeking answers to. So you, as practitioner, have to listen to their words and their silences, observe their facial expressions, gestures, and movements and pay attention to the marks or things they make.

TRY YOUR HAND

Below are some vignettes of children at work and play. Try and analyse them in terms of what you think the children are interested in or what theories they are constructing. Then say how you might respond.

The first is an account of four children discovering a bug.

Samu and Giorgio are playing with the blocks when they see a bug. Samu says, 'It's not moving. Look it's not moving any part of its body.'

Giorgio says, 'I don't like it. It could sting me even with my pants still on.'

Oliver tries to sweep up the bug using the small brush and shovel from the sand tray. He taps the bug and listens to the sound the tapping makes.

Angie starts to draw the bug, using dark coloured crayons and mixing the colours carefully as she works.

Compare your responses with the possibilities suggested below.

- Did you think that Samu is considering the possibility that the bug might be dead? This is often the great unasked question because death continues to be a fascinating and still rather a taboo area. Might you be tempted to follow up by asking him if he thinks it is dead and be willing to engage with him and the other children about death?
- You will have recognised that Giorgio is scared of being stung. Would you ask him and the other children if they have ever been stung by a bug or another creature and possibly develop the little scenario into a project around stinging creatures? Or talk about fears more broadly? Or think about making a collection of bugs? Or even getting the children to invent and illustrate a bug of their own?
- Both Samu and Giorgio create protonarratives about what they have experienced and use this as a way of communicating their thoughts and fears. How might you use this – the structuring of everyday events into logical tales – to take their learning forward?
- Oliver's response seems to me a very socially responsible one. He realises that the others are not keen to have the bug close to them so he finds a way to move it and then taps on its shell and listens to the sound it makes. Perhaps he is asking what the shell is made of, if it is hard or not and what purpose it serves. His actions show his ability to empathise with the anxieties or dislikes of others. Would you comment on this to help him know what he has done and why it matters? And how might you take

his obvious interest in materials further? Perhaps collect things that make different sounds when tapped, when plucked, when blown?

- Angie tries to represent the bug, paying attention to the colours of its shell. Perhaps she is experimenting with ways of making a particular colour. How might you support her in doing this by thinking about the resources available?

Malaguzzi said that what children learn is often not what teachers set out to teach them. What they learn arises from being able to follow their own interests accompanied by the helpful responses teachers and practitioners make in recognition of this.

The emphasis is on the child as initiator and the interaction is only successful for the child's learning when the adult can respond appropriately, sometimes verbally or with physical help, or offering resources, or in other ways. How educators respond is totally dependent on their active listening.

Kate Pahl (1999) looked at children in both a nursery setting and at home and used close observation as the tool for gathering evidence about their early literacy development. This was a research project and so she had a set of questions she was going to ask and devised a way for her project to work:

- She chose to observe children in a nursery class where her own child was a pupil. In making this choice she ensured that the children would see her not as an outsider but as a parent who often came in and worked with them. She became a *participant observer* which means she joined in whilst observing.
- During her time in the nursery (2 hours per week) she recorded everything that happened and took away some of the models and drawings made by the children or took photographs of what they produced.
- She watched the children and made brief notes, which she then took home and wrote up in more detail. These became her observation notes or her working notes.
- What she did next is very important. She read through the notes again and again and thought about what they told her or showed her about the children's developing understanding of literacy.

17

Let's remember that she had a particular focus, which was to understand more about children's development in literacy. To do this she became a participant observer, recorded everything she heard and saw, kept notes which she later read and reflected on in light of her knowledge about the acquisition of literacy. We begin to see a process emerging which shows just how the thinking observer uses observation as a valid and important educational tool. Pahl based her observation techniques on assuming that everything a child says or does is significant in building up a picture of her understanding of the world. This is similar to what **Clifford Geertz** called 'thick description'. He believed that in order to understand a culture all aspects of that culture needed to be understood. I am saying that in order to understand the children in your group you need to know as much as possible about each child and to do this you may need to involve the views of your colleagues, the child herself, parents and carers, other people who interact with the child and more.

A SET OF KEY QUESTIONS

Through recording what is seen and heard we begin to be able to ask and answer some vital questions. You might want to keep a note of these because they are useful to anyone involved in observing children:

- What is this child paying attention to or interested in? How do I know or how can I find out?
- What experience does the child have of this? How do I know? And how can I find out? Who might I need to consult?
- What does the child already know about this? How do I know?
- What does the child feel about this? How do I know?

I used these questions to analyse Ben's list of countries. When he was a very little boy he wrote out a list of the names of countries he had heard of, using his developing understanding of the English written system. When his list was complete he asked me, 'Can you read them?'

sthaFGR
TUCe
UmeRC
Venom
itaL
FRDS

Since he is my grandson I already knew a lot about him and his experiences throughout his life. This prior knowledge put me at an advantage so that when I read his list several fascinating things emerged. First was that he drew together his current interest in writing lists of all sorts (see below) with his interest in beginning to be able to work out how to write words in English. Second was that the countries he had chosen to list all had some personal significance for him. He was born in South Africa and at the time he wrote the list his father was on holiday there. He had had a lovely holiday in the summer in the next country on the list – Turkey. America was much in the news because of 9/11 at the time and his best friend at school had missed the start of term because he was in Vietnam. He has spent holidays in Italy and has friends who sometimes go to France.

I used the questions above and this is what I concluded.

Ben used a combination of lower and upper case letters and a combination of the sounds he thinks a letter makes and the sound of the name of the letter, as shown in TUCe, which you will have realised says Turkey. He knows or suspects that the words he writes are not always correct, but is delighted that people like me might be able to read them. He knows that some lists are written vertically as a column, and that writing means creating something that others can read. I would also suggest that he is confident enough to label his list as a set of countries, to invite me to read it and to show off about some of the countries he has heard of

A few weeks after producing the list of countries Ben produced a sheaf of small pieces of paper, on each of which was written the name of one of the children in his class. Here he was using the concept of listing but organising it differently onto individual pieces of paper. Was he exploring whether a list has to be linear or whether it is still a list if it appears on separate pieces of paper? We can guess: only Ben knows the answer.

If we can learn so much about children through observing them, might not they learn as much from observing both the adults around them and one another? We mentioned the work of Barbara Rogoff earlier in this book. You will recall that she observed children learning about the cultures in which they live through *their* observations of skilled adults or more skilled children. In most of the situations cited in her research the adults make no effort to 'teach' the children but the children themselves take responsibility for working out the essential features of an activity, and accommodating this into their existing understanding. This feature of children being the agents of their own learning – and doing this by watching what others do and then having a go – is also commented on by researchers in the developing world.

TRY YOUR HAND

The example below is drawn from Rogoff's work. Read it and suggest what you think the child learns from the interaction.

A Mayan toddler in Guatemala, going with his mother to the market, watches and listens as she bargains for a good price for a cabbage.

What did you say about what the child has learned from this everyday experience? Rogoff says that this child is learning about his mother's role within their lived lives and about the custom adults learn, culture, conventions and ways of doing things, particularly with regard to money and food.

Observation, then, is a tool for learning to be used in many settings and by many people. Sometimes learners cannot only observe but participate in the process, as in Guatemala where **Nash** (1967) reports that adults learning to weave merely sit alongside a skilled weaver, asking no questions and being given no explanations. The learner may be asked to fetch a spool of thread but does not begin to weave until he or she feels competent to do so. At that point the apprentice becomes the skilled weaver. What this suggests is that skilled observation is an active and not a passive learning process. It is worth thinking about what, if any, opportunities we offer to children to become skilled observers themselves.

MOVING ON

The first chapter addressed some of the things adults need to know about how children learn and develop. This chapter adds to this but shifts the focus to the ways and things we observe when in interaction with children and begins to consider how to *interpret* what we see and hear in terms of what we know. Interpreting what is seen and heard refers to the questions we ask and answer as we try to make sense of our observations.

Chapter 3

Documenting learning

At nearly 4 months Hannah turned to examine whoever was talking; smiled in anticipation when Sam started chanting 'The Owl and the Pussy Cat'; and when an adult counted '1, 2, 3 . . .' she waited with closed eyes in anticipation of the thrill of whatever would follow.

This comes from the first and only *developmental diary* I kept of the development of one child. When my own children were born I was too young, too ignorant, too nervous and definitely too tired to do anything other than love them and care for them. They seemed just babies to me. But when my first grandchild was born I had developed an intense interest in and knowledge of early learning and development. So I watched this little baby and kept a very primitive sort of developmental diary, based on photographs I took of her and observations I made. At the time I did not know that diaries like this have charted individual development by such legendary figures as Charles Darwin amongst others. I kept my observation notes for the first 6 months of Hannah's life. Here are some of the notes I made and below each an analysis of what I thought theorists might say about what the observation showed about Hannah's learning.

At 12 weeks Sam, her mother, said that Hannah had, by accident, hit the bell attached to an elephant mobile over her cot. She then repeated this action again and again, sometimes smiling at the bell and sometimes crying.

It is tempting to think about this in fairly simple terms. By accident the child's foot rang the bell. The child liked the sound of the bell ringing and kept kicking out to try and make the same thing happen again. That seems plausible, but something is missing from that analysis. In order for Hannah to keep kicking she must have realised that it was her physical actions that caused the bell to ring. In other words she must have had a sense of her own *agency* – her ability to make things happen in her immediate environment. And we are talking here of a child less than 3 months old.

> At more or less the same time, a friend of mine came to see the new baby and brought with her her own 5-year-old child, Jess – the first child Hannah had encountered. She sat on Jess's lap and really looked at the pictures in a book when Jess read it and at one point laughed out loud.

Here is Hannah in *interaction* with another child – the first small being she had encountered. Jess was an 'expert other' in terms of already knowing about how books work, what people do with them and what enchantments they offer. So she knew to open the book and turn the pages and say the words and point to the pictures. Vygotsky would have said that the more expert child mediated the younger child's understanding of the world through the use of a cultural tool, a book.

Here are two brief pieces from the developmental diaries kept by Charles Darwin. You will see how much more analytical and perceptive they are than my grandmotherly diaries. Darwin not only travelled the world and developed the theory of the origin of the species, but managed to keep detailed diaries of the development of all of his many children. I managed a 6-month diary for only one of my grandchildren! But both sets of diaries are detailed observations made in order to try and understand more about an individual infant.

> When seven weeks old, his eyes were attracted by a dangling tassel & a bright colour. This was shewn by his eyes becoming fixed & the movements of his arms ceasing. Emma argues that his smiles were from seeing her face, because a tassel dangling did not make him smile – it is afterwards remarked that his smiles generally, or at least very frequently are merely from an inward pleasure, with no relation to anything external . . . The day after this he was not quite well & did not smile the whole day, which shews I think that the smiles on the previous days did express pleasure. The movement of his arms I have before said appeared to be without any object, but this exception must

be made that from his earliest days he could easily find his way to his mouth with his hand, when he wanted to suck.

Nine weeks old – During the last week & more it is remarkable how his eyes have brightened when smiling – often accompanied by a little noise, approaching to a laugh.

(http://www.darwinproject.ac.uk/observations-
on-children, accessed 31 December 2014)

Developmental diaries are a recognised and accepted way of recording what is seen in minute detail, analysing it and arriving at some under-standings. You will find many examples in the literature including many charting how young children acquire language.

WHO IS THIS DOCUMENTATION FOR?

There are several reasons and audiences for documenting progress. Parents and carers will want to know how well their children are doing away from the home. They continually take notice of their children and are attentive to significant moments, sometimes called milestones. In the case of very young children where parents need or want to start or return to work they may fear they will miss out on significant moments in their child's learning and development – the first word, the first step and so on. In the asili nidi (creches) for the youngest children in Reggio Emilia daily records of personal events are displayed where the parents can see them. These often include photographs of the babies and toddlers taken during the day but also written notes about when the baby slept, what she ate, together with anything unusual or interesting that she said, did or made. On one of my visits to an asilo nido one of the parents said that she found the information about when her child had slept and what she had eaten very helpful in knowing what to offer the child when back at home.

Another said that she had no idea that her child was so good at making marks on paper. *Cameras and written notes* make up this documentation.

Work displayed around the room where the children play and learn is an informative and often delightful way of documenting their progress and is meant for the children themselves to celebrate their own work and that of their peers, for other workers in the setting to notice what children in other groups can do and for parents and carers to look at when they come into the setting. You may know that the preschools in Reggio Emilia are famous for the quality of the artwork produced by the children. This is largely due to the fact that there is a studio or atelier in each one where an artist works during the day and children come in to watch or join in. A visit to one of their settings is almost like a visit to an art gallery. This is a lovely thing to witness but not necessarily something you will seek to emulate in your own setting when one considers the difference there is in the status of and funding for early childhood education there and here.

TRY YOUR HAND

In terms of documenting progress analyse the different ways in which an identical piece of work (such as Figure 3.1) could be displayed and think about how informative each one is.

Figure 3.1

Example 1: Put up on the wall with the child's name attached.

Example 2: Put up on the wall with the child's name and the date on which it had been completed together with the label 'Hannah's musical instruments'.

Example 3: Put up on the wall together with the label 'Hannah is learning to play the violin and she is learning to write. Here is some work she did on her own as she thought about all the musical instruments she knows about. Can you read her labels and see what she already knows about how to write words?'

This tiny scrap of work does not, in itself, say a lot about the person who produced it. So just labelling it with the child's name or even giving it a title is not very informative. But contextualising it – giving it a narrative – really helps the viewer to analyse what the child was paying attention to and interested in, what she already knows and what she might be offered next to take her learning forward. Example 3 is clearly the most informative but is it doable when you have a class of more than 20 children?

Computers and other digital electronic devices can play an important role in documenting progress and are being used more and more widely in many settings in many countries. With your mobile phone or tablet you are able to record short sequences of film, able to capture what is said and done by a group of children – something that was really difficult to do in the past. These devices make the actual recording simpler. But the task of analysing what you see remains the same. It requires you to analyse in light of what you know about the child and about child development.

Here is an example drawn from the work in Reggio Emilia where using technology with very young children is part and parcel of everyday life in the preschools. At *La Villetta* School in Reggio Emilia the teachers often took the children out into the city to explore its urban and green spaces, its streets and squares, homes and shops, parks and garden. After a particularly late rainy season the adults had noticed that the children had been talking about the effect of rain on their city. They wondered how some familiar and new places would look in and after the rain. They said it would be a good idea to take photographs before and after the rain. The late rains were offering the children a lot of time to think about what materials and tools they would need in order to ask and answer their questions. They decided which would need cameras and a printer; they thought of things they might collect or measure or record. They gathered and compared their questions: How deep would the puddles be? What things might float on them? What things would be reflected in them? What new things might grow? When the rainstorm first broke the children were very excited and noticed things no one had anticipated. They noticed that people changed their speed and posture when walking in the rain; the shiny streets and reflections changed the familiar and made it seem quite strange; raindrops made different sounds when falling on the pavement from falling on the cars or on leaves on the trees. They began to draw and paint, make stories, design waterproof clothing, measure the depth of puddles, collect things that floated and those that sank. They fashioned trees in clay and tried to make them look wet. The project became known as the City in the Rain and was documented by Forman in his chapter called 'The use of digital media in Reggio Emilia'. By digital media Forman is talking of things like computers, CDs, printers, scanners, digital cameras, digital video recorders and players, tablets and other devices. The children drew their ideas on large poster paper. Some drew their theories of the rain's source: 'The devil makes it rain,' said one 5-year-old. Another insisted that 'The rain is made by big machines in the sky, and the rain goes into the clouds, and when the clouds are too full the rain falls out.' The initial drawings were the children's first theories about the rain cycle and they served as a platform from which to discuss and expand the children's understanding. The project continued for many weeks and included the children making audiotapes of the sounds of the rain on different surfaces and then making a graphic representation of that; drawing a system of water works that bring the rain water from the sky to the ground then into pipes into homes; using a sequence of photographs that show a changing sky followed by drawing these changes on paper; drawing a city before, during and after a rainfall. And much more, all using their hundred languages (drawn on Forman 2012, in Edwards *et al.* 2012: 348–55).

The last example of this kind of observation where the adult is recording in some way and analysing what is recorded comes from New Zealand where Margaret Carr and her colleagues developed a system which they called *learning stories*. These are nothing more than a set of observations made over time within the ordinary day to day activities and events of the setting – a collection of what Carr calls snapshots. But there is an underpinning philosophy to the collection and that is that the observations are focused on what Carr refers to as the five target domains or *learning dispositions*. To understand this we need to define what a disposition is. My definition is rather different from that of Carr. For me a disposition is a tendency or a habit of mind. Here I draw on discussions

I had with the great American early childhood thinker, Lilian Katz, who said that a disposition is a pattern of behaviour which is often exhibited in the absence of any coercion. So it is a habit of mind which might be oriented to broad goals, some good and some less so. So a child could have a disposition towards becoming a reader or a disposition to be disruptive in the setting. For Margaret Carr the dispositions are described by actions, as follow:

- taking an interest;
- being involved;
- persisting in the case of difficulty or uncertainty;
- expressing ideas or feelings;
- taking responsibility or accepting the views of other people.

You need to know that Carr sees these dispositions as being sequential (rather like Piaget's view of stages) and moving from taking an interest to taking responsibility.

TRY YOUR HAND

Here are some learning stories from 4-year-old Amir. Analyse how what he says and does represents one or more of Carr's dispositions.

- *Amir's attention was drawn to a car accident he had witnessed on his way to school. He talked about it all day, to the children and the adults and drew several pictures of it.*
- *Amir's mum has been trying to get him to fasten his own shoes using the velcro fastening. After playing outside he took off his shoes and then put them on and fastened them and repeated this several times.*
- *'My mum was really cross with me this morning because I didn't eat my cereal. The milk didn't taste good and I told my mum but she said not to fuss. So I threw the bowl on the floor. And boy! Was my mum mad at me then!'*
- *When Amir's friend Chantelle hurt herself in the garden he brought her inside to tell one of the adults and explained, 'She just fell. It wasn't me. I wasn't even playing with her.'*

How did your analysis of this go? My analysis is that the first shows that this child certainly takes an interest in something that has happened and can also express his feelings through both talking about the event and drawing it. The second shows him able to persist in doing something he had previously struggled with. The third shows his ability to share his ideas and take responsibility for what had happened. The last story shows him again taking responsibility for something good that he had done.

It is up to you to decide how helpful this approach might be to you. Personally, I love the stories but am not sure that the five dispositions help the analysis.

MOVING ON

In this chapter we have looked at different ways of taking notice of what children say and do and paid some attention to using these bits of evidence to arrive at some conclusion about what the child knows and can do. It is an approach where you, the adult, are assessing what you have seen and heard in terms of what you know about the individual child based on some understanding of child development. You are looking at what the child did today compared with what the child could do when last you looked. There are no standards or norms or targets or stages. We move on, in the next chapter, to a more serious and in-depth critique of assessment in schools and settings.

Chapter 4

Assessing and understanding learning

I had hoped to open this chapter by quoting the whole letter written by the sadly missed writer and educationalist Ted Wragg, who viewed all the insane and meaningless innovations in education through the eyes of a clear thinker, a fair critic and an honest judge of sense versus nonsense. The letter I had wanted to use was printed in the *Guardian* of Tuesday 1 June 2004 and was entitled 'The lunacy of reception-class tickboxes'. It arose when Ofsted criticised the assessment procedures for children in the Foundation Stage in England.

I am not able to quote the entire letter but will summarise it as best I can, including snippets that cannot be left out because they are so wonderful. Wragg started the piece by telling readers that his response to the Ofsted report, critical of the new planned assessment procedures of the day, was one of the utmost glee. He wanted to turn cartwheels in the street. In an earlier *Guardian* article ('Wise words', *Guardian*, 9 July 2002) he had railed at the introduction of what he called '*the wretched thing*' which required that reception class teachers assess children on 13 scales, each with 9 different statements: in total making 117 judgements for each 4- and 5-year-old child in the class. If you can be bothered to do the maths you will see that, for a class of 30 children, the poor teacher will make a grand total of 3,510 assessments each term.

So Wragg protested about the size of the task but more than that about the meaninglessness of the task.

> Many of the tickboxes are ludicrous. Some are brainlessly vague, such as 'maintains attention and concentrates' (on what, for goodness sake – setting fire to the wendy house?). The item 'reads books of own choice with some fluency and accuracy' fails to distinguish between Little Twinky and War and Peace, while 'uses everyday words to

describe position' presumably earns a tick for both "'ere' and '45 degrees east north-east of Samarkand'.

More seriously Wragg questioned if it was possible for anyone to make a proper judgement of such things as how well such a young child could be judged on the capacity to show respect for her culture and beliefs and those of others. Having made a judgement the poor harassed teacher had then to discuss the judgements with the parents. How on earth can you explain to a parent why you have judged their child as being unable to tell right from wrong?

Here is what Wragg says about the requirement to assess creative development, taking as an example the learning goal which goes like this:

'Expresses feelings and preferences in response to artwork, drama and music and makes some comparisons and links between different pieces. Responds to own work and that of others when exploring and communicating ideas, feelings and preferences throughout art, music, dance, role-play and imaginative play'. Er . . . yes, give him a tick. Hold on . . . maybe no. Too undiscriminating on tambourine technique and lack of empathy when pretending to be a potted plant.

For nearly 2 years this assessment regime has been forced on children and their teachers – children who should have been exploring, experimenting, questioning, creating theories, making and learning; teachers who should have been spending their time listening to the children, supporting them, getting to know them and enjoying teaching them but instead have had to follow them around with clipboards merely to satisfy the needs of mad statisticians in the DfES.

The last word goes to Wragg:

All protests have been completely ignored. Even a damning report from Ofsted will be easily brushed aside. No problem, guv, a little tweak here and there will suffice. And in the totalitarian society in which we now live there is absolutely nothing anyone can do about it. Except vomit.

The requirements for assessing children in the early years in this country have changed, been slimmed down and simplified – all to be celebrated – but now require not only children in the reception class but children as young as 2 years old to be assessed.

TRY YOUR HAND

On the page that follows you can find an example of the sort of assessment being proposed for children between the ages of 2 and 3 years. It is not dreadful, but it raises serious issues and questions about why practitioners are being required to complete this. Think about the following issues and questions:

Who decides what a 2-year-old should know and be able to do?

Are all 2-year-olds the same in terms of their experience and interests?

If there is no everybaby (meaning that we can talk about babies as though they are all the same) can we accept that there is an everytoddler?

DEFINING ASSESSMENT

Assessment is a loaded word and has meanings relating to evaluating different things. It is really important to remember that it is not the same as testing or examining. We talk about assessing a child's progress in school as well as a school's position up a league table. We assess how well we are teaching or how successful we feel we are as parents. We assess the state of our finances and make decisions on the basis of this. In this book we are thinking about how we can evaluate the learning and development of the children in our care. We want to know that each child is learning and developing and we want to know what it is that is helping this learning. So we are talking about a *process* – the process of *making a judgement* or coming to a conclusion about a child or children after a *careful examination of the evidence* and *in light of our knowledge of child development*. I have put the key words or phrases in italics to emphasise them. They are essential to a real understanding of assessment. If you think about it you will see that in the previous chapter about observation and documentation we have been talking about gathering the evidence.

You may find it helpful to think about assessment as being a scientific process. You will know that science is essentially evidence-based and nowadays we talk of medicine being evidence-based, conclusions about global warming being evidence-based and so on. Testing a child on a one-off or occasional basis, or ticking a box offers no evidence. These actions are, at best, the end product of a process which may have used evidence but the evidence is not public and freely available. Children's work, examples of what they have said and done, by contrast, are evidence and accessible to others (see Table 4.1).

Let's try and redefine what assessment is and why it is important. As educators and practitioners we have a responsibility to ensure that the children in our care are making progress in their journey from dependence to independence in all aspects of learning and development. The best way of knowing that is to gather evidence as part of the normal daily life. This can be in the form of notes jotted down by you and your colleagues, examples of what the child has said and done, photographs, video clips, actual things the child has made and so on, all dated and, where possible, annotated. In the days before target setting became a national passion, collecting this evidence into a file or a book for each child was common and good practice. And it is still done in many countries of the world.

Figure 4.1 is an example taken from my book *A Guide to Early Years Practice* showing how one adult selected a piece of drawing and writing, analysed it and wrote her comment on the evidence.

On the day after her fourth birthday, Farida wrote her name in full and drew herself with a body, both for the first time. She also wrote the number four.

Figure 4.1

Table 4.1

A Unique Child

Early Years Foundation Stage
Learning and Development Summary

Name *Angus*   Date *01 January 201x*   Age *2 years and 4 months*

A child learning	Personal, Social and Emotional Development

A child learning

Playing and exploring
Finding out and exploring; playing with what they know; Being willing to have a go.

Active learning
Being involved and concentrating; Enjoying achieving what they set out to do; Keeping on trying.

Creating and thinking critically
Having their own ideas; Making links; Choosing ways to do things.

Angus is keen to explore everything in nursery. He's especially likes being outside – his favourite lately is turning over logs to see creatures underneath – this holds his attention for a long time. He's started looking carefully along the ground in other places, like along the base of the shed. He also loves to dig on the mud patch. Angus likes to move, and lately he has been more willing to climb and to keep trying even when its difficult for him.

Personal, Social and Emotional Development
Self-confidence and self awareness;
Making relationships; Managing feelings and behavior

He has wanted daddy to stay for a short while and read him a story before he leaves him over the past few weeks, but he soon settles with a cuddle on the sofa. He explores everything in nursery with interest and seeks to do things for himself. He asks for help when he needs it. He plays with other children and usually accepts fitting in with routines with encouragement, though sometimes he gets upset needs support to calm down if things dont go his way.

Self-confidence and self-awareness

0–11	8–20	16–26	(22-36)	30–50	40–60+

Making relationships

0–11	8–20	16–26	(22-36)	30–50	40–60+

Managing feelings and behavior

0–11	8–20	(16–26)	22–36	30–50	40–60+

Communication and Language
Listening and attention; Understanding; Speaking

Angus communicates confidently, both with children and adults, and is acquiring new words all the time. He is putting words together to explain things – I doned it, at the door!
Enjoys sitting one to one with a book – likes to whizz through them quickly and prefers to talk about and point to the pictures than to hear a story read. He points to the pictures or answers a question like 'who's that?' or 'Where's the ball?'.

Physical development
Moving and handling; Health and self-care

Physical skills have continued to develop well. Angus is more confident on the climbing frame – and he recently enjoyed the mini trampoline and throwing and rolling hoops and balls in the garden – lots of laughing. He also enjoyed the manipulating small pieces of natural materials such as lentils, lavender, rice and twigs to create and glue – was quite absorbed in this.

Listening and attention

0–11	8–20	16–26	(22-36)	30–50	40–60+

Understanding

0–11	8–20	16–26	(22-36)	30–50	40–60+	Moving and handling					

Moving and handling

0–11	8–20	16–26	22–36	30–50	40–60+

Speaking

0–11	8–20	16–26	(22-36)	30–50	40–60+

Health and self-care

0–11	8–20	16–26	22–36	30–50	40–60+

Next steps to support learning and development:
Continue to support Angus's language development through activities and during daily routines, in order to build his vocabulary further.
Use short stories and factual books to support his interest in worms, creepy crawlies and gardens.
Ask daddy to take home books from the library.
Continue to offer a range of physical opportunities to build confidence – including using he soft play resources and begin to introduce mathematical language in a practical way while using these.

Parent(s) signature(s)/comment	**Key Person signature**
Angus has a new brother, Theo, who is two months old now – he is excited and spends lots of time with him – but is a bit more clingy when I bring him to nursery. We know he loves coming to nursery.	**Moderated by**

Source: © earlylearningconsultancy.co.uk.

http://www.foundationyears.org.uk/files/2012/03/A-Know-How-Guide.pdf, accessed 31 December 2014

ASSESSING CHILDREN IN TERMS OF MEETING PRE-DETERMINED CRITERIA

In today's world, however, children are required to meet targets and you may be required to record whether they do or not. The targets that are set for children in our education system are based on assumptions made about what children of different ages should know and be able to do. You will appreciate that this ties them firmly to Piaget's age/stage ideas of development and takes no account of later findings about how learning is continuous, social, context-bound, not limited to critical periods and immensely individual. Some children learn more quickly than others. Some children learn much about things that interest them and little about things that don't. To claim, for example, that all 2-year-olds should be able to say sentences made up of more than 4 words is as senseless as stating that all infants should sit unaided by the age of 3 months.

If you had to state what you think that the majority of children should know and be able to do at the age of 2 or 3 or 4 or 5 you would have enormous difficulty because so much depends on the make up and experience of each child. And so much depends on what you think it is important for children to know. I gathered some responses from colleagues and students to the question you have just been asked but added to it that they should think about all aspects of learning and development – physical, linguistic, cognitive, creative, personal, scientific, problem solving and reasoning, social and emotional.

TRY YOUR HAND

Write down your thoughts on what you believe young children should know and be able to do by the time they enter the reception class/formal schooling, thinking about intellectual development, personal, social and emotional development, physical development, emotional development, how they are able to express their ideas, and how they set about solving problems. Now read what some other people said in response to this question and compare your answer to theirs.

Amalia said: 'I would want all children to be confident to express their ideas and thoughts to somebody else in their first language. I would want them to love listening to stories and rhymes and to spend time looking at books. I would want them to be curious and ask questions and try things out. I would want to see them solving problems relating to everyday experiences like setting the table in the home corner using the same number of cups as saucers, for example, or using the play money when shopping. I would expect them to be able to take turns and share (not all the time, of course) and to show interest in other children and the ability to sense what they are feeling. Physically? Well, run and jump and climb and ride a tricycle, to use fine motor skills to make marks and tools.'

Ben said: 'Well, all children should be able to keep their curiosity and get very involved in doing things that interest them. They should know how to ask for help when they need it and they should be able to get on with other children and with adults. I like to see them show a range of emotions because to only ever seem happy seems not normal to me. So I expect them to show anger and fear and hope and love and joy.'

Sizwe said: 'They must build on what they know and have experienced to have a solid base for everything. They should be part of a community and able to communicate there and to take turns and make decisions and participate fully in many things. But they can also want to be alone or want to be quiet. I want for all children what I want for my own – to be full, equal and respected members of their learning community, their family community and neighbourhood community.'

Archana said: 'I suppose they should be able to read simple books, write their own name and some simple words. They should be able to count to . . . 20? or maybe more. They should be able to climb the climbing frame, ride a trike, use pen and pencil and paintbrush and scissors. They should be able to copy patterns and have begun to write neatly. They should be able to control their feelings and not get into fights.'

Noreen said: 'I want to see the child as continuing to be a competent, questioning, communicative, engaged, emotional, expressive member of a community of learners. I want to see a move from dependence to independence and willingness to take risks, make mistakes, evaluate and start again. The early years should be laying the foundations for each child to move on in life carrying these positive dispositions with her. What more can one ask for?'

How did you get on? I imagine that you agreed with some of these because most are very general and they are the sort of goals we might have for our own children. But how are you going to measure what you see and hear against something as broad as 'be part of a community', or 'participate fully'? Archana takes the narrowest view and states things that are measurable – able to read, count to 20, climb the climbing frame. You can tick each of these boxes. Policy makers in many countries set about this daunting task by trying to break down these broad and generally unmeasurable attributes into goals or targets. Some do it very well but others – for example the original Foundation Stage targets slated by Wragg – went into minute detail creating a monster of box-ticking that was more than onerous for practitioners and largely meaningless to others.

TEACHING TO THE TARGET

Do you think that a child who is regularly assessed against a whole set of targets will make more progress than a child who is never formally assessed? The answer to this is clearly no: as the old saying goes 'weighing the pig does not make it fatter'. Testing children and being obsessed with goals and targets, scores and ratings means that the quality of the education on offer may suffer as practitioners start to teach to the targets rather than to teach to the children's interests and needs. Good early years practice always starts with the interests of the children, allows the children to get deeply involved in what they are doing and the adults with them to take careful notice of what they do and say so that their learning can be noted, consolidated and extended.

MOVING ON

In the next chapter we think about how you, the practitioner/educator, can help children move on in their learning. You will know how important this part of your role is as you help the child move on from being able to do something initially with help to being able to do it alone.

Chapter 5

Extending children's learning

> Even when I listened to the children I did not use their ideas. I paid attention only long enough to adapt their words to my plans.
>
> (Vivian Gussin Paley 1929: 8)

We have already looked at what you, the practitioner, needs to know about children and their development and at how evidence of children's learning can be gathered and analysed. We now look at how what children have shown us that they can do can be explicitly recognised and used to help them move on as independent learners. To do this we need some more theory.

THE ZONE OF PROXIMAL DEVELOPMENT

We will start by returning to Vygotsky. He was interested in observing and analysing how children make progress. He noted that children move from everyday concepts (the things they discover in their exploration of their real worlds) to scientific or more abstract concepts, and from using cultural tools like making notes or drawing pictures to enable and enhance memory to using internalised memory for solving problems. For him this charted how children become able to *internalise experiences* in order to remember them and develop high order cognitive skills. He realised that teachers were often teaching children the things they already knew and could do. He was not thinking about early childhood here because, as I am sure you know, early childhood practitioners rarely teach in any formal way. But his thoughts are relevant in that they remind us that we need to know what children can already do in order to help them move on.

So he postulated the idea of a notional gap – what we might call a virtual gap in today's language – between what the child could do alone and what the child might do with help. He called it the *Zone of Proximal Development* (ZPD). It is the gap between what the child can do alone and what the child might be able to do with help: a gap between the *performance level* and the *potential level*. Vygotsky (1977: 96) wrote: '*In play a child is always above his average age, above his daily behavior; in play it is as though he were a head taller than himself . . . in play it is as though the child were trying to jump above the level of his normal behavior.*' He was talking particularly about imaginative play but his words remind us that play is a primary mode or way of learning, especially in the early years and watching a child at play gives you a real insight into what they can already do alone as well as what they might do with help.

TRY YOUR HAND

Mary Smith was a student when I knew her and she was just starting to keep detailed observation notes of the children in her Under Fives Centre. Here is an extract from one of these observation notes and the question I am asking you to consider is what Daniel (4 years and 6 months) knew and could do. The children were in the garden in springtime looking at a small swarm of bees that had arrived.

Daniel . . . started talking about making honey. He said we could make some at the nursery. I asked him how we could do it. He replied that we had to pick some flowers together. We went inside to get a tray for the flowers, then back to the garden to collect wild flowers – daisies, buttercups and dandelions. When the tray was full we sat on the grass and studied them. Daniel said, 'We have to pick out the pollen from the centre of each flower.' It took a while to do this, placing it in the corner of the tray. Daniel said we had enough to make the honey and then asked me to go get a cup and spoon. I got them. Daniel put the contents into the cup and then stirred it with the spoon saying, 'I know it will make honey!'

After a time I asked, 'What's happening to it, Daniel?' 'Nothing,' he replied, 'we have to add apple juice to it and then it will be honey!'

This is how I analysed this example. Daniel is an articulate child and has some knowledge about nature. He talked about pollen and used the word 'centre' rather than 'middle', which impressed me. He developed several theories and was prepared to change them when it was clear that they did not apply. He was very persistent and determined to achieve his goal. He clearly had some experience of both bees and honey. Up to this point Daniel has not been able to make honey, even with the help of the adult.

SCAFFOLDING LEARNING

Bruner was very interested in how children learn but also concerned at how many young children appear to fail in formal educational settings. He started to analyse what happened to the infant learner within the home and compare that with the child learner in a school or setting. At home the infant is alongside a caregiver, often the mother, and their interactions take place around the everyday events of the home. Almost every exchange involves everyday concepts and makes human sense to the child. This is not necessarily the case in exchanges in settings where children are often asked to do things that do not make human sense to them — where they cannot see the purpose. After all, does it make human sense to colour all the squares red and all the circles green? Like Vygotsky he saw all learning as social and rooted in culture and he saw all children learning from expert others, children or adults.

Knowing about the ZPD he began to think about just what it was that successful teachers/practitioners do to take learning forward and he noticed that they pay careful attention to what children are doing and saying and then intervene in some way to make the child think about what to do next.

TRY YOUR HAND

Now go back to the example of Daniel and read what happened next.

I got the apple juice from the kitchen. Daniel poured it into the cup and stirred, saying 'Is it honey now?'

'No,' I replied. 'I don't think people can make honey . . . only bees.' Daniel was not convinced and said, 'We have to put more pollen in and then it will be honey.'

We added more, but couldn't make honey. At this point I said, 'Daniel, we've tried our best to make honey but people can't make it. We'll look for a book about bees and that will show us how they make it.'

We found a book and sat for a long time reading, looking and explaining – page by page. As a follow up we went to the shop to buy honey and even managed to get a jar with honeycomb in it. The children enjoyed the experience of spreading the honey on rolls and eating them at tea time.

Can you say just what it was that made this practitioner a supportive educator in the sense of helping Daniel move on in his learning? Think about what Daniel learned and how Mary enabled him to learn.

What Mary did was complicated and sensitive.

- She was genuinely interested in what he was saying and what he wanted to do.
- She followed up all his ideas as an equal partner getting the apple juice when he asked for it and helping add pollen.
- She made suggestions about how to move on from not having been able to make honey by first sharing a book about bees (a cultural tool) with him and then suggesting going to the shop to buy honey.

She *scaffolded* his learning. Scaffolding was the term used by Bruner for a process whereby the more expert other in any interaction is able to support the child's learning just as a scaffold supports a building whilst it is being erected. Doing this enables the child to move from dependence on help to independence.

SUSTAINED SHARED THINKING

The *Researching Effective Pedagogy in the Early Years* project, led by Iram Siraj-Blatchford, Kathy Sylva, Stella Muttock, Rose Gilden and Danny Bell, set out to try and identify what enabled the practice in fourteen settings found by the earlier *Effective Provision for Pre-School Education* to be described as high quality. What they found will not surprise you. The most important factor was the *quality of adult–child interactions*. In these settings the children were making the best progress and the activities were based on offering children many varied hands-on, direct experiences where children could draw on their prior experience and come to new understandings. In the views of the researchers what characterised the quality they identified was the evidence of *opportunities for children to become deeply involved in meaningful activities together with adults, both sharing meaning and engaged with understanding one another.* There are some key words and phrases in this sentence including deeply involved, meaningful activities, together with, sharing meaning, understanding one another. The researchers said that the learning that took place through these interventions was particular in what they called *sustained shared thinking* between a pair (or a *dyad*) of learner and adult. In their views this adds to the concept of scaffolding and can be said to be an activity where:

- The adult pays attention to what the child is doing or wanting to do, and has sufficient knowledge of her own in terms of the subject or activity involved. This is essential if she is to respond appropriately to the child. So it involves both the child's awareness of what is to be learned and the adult's assessment of what is 'required' for the child to succeed.

- The active co-construction of an idea or a skill. By co-construction they mean that the adult and child do this together.

INTERSUBJECTIVITY

Fourteen-month-old Malika crawled over to her toy box and took out every toy. She then looked at her mother and started to cry. 'What is it you want?' asked her mother, going over to the box to see if she could identify what it was the baby could clearly not find. She saw the arm of a doll sticking out from underneath the rug and held it up. 'Is this it?' A big smile was both the answer to her question and a reward for her perseverance.

This is an easy to analyse and everyday occurrence. Parents and carers and educators of very young children have to find ways of guessing what it is the child wants or is doing or is trying to find out in order to meet the child's needs. For learning to take place there must be a sharing of meaning and purpose. As you will know by now this takes place through what Vygotsky called *intersubjectivity* which means the shared meanings that people construct through their interactions with one another as they use cultural tools to interpret aspects of their social, cultural or intellectual lives. Shared cognition (or thinking) and agreement are essential ingredients in learning. Vygotsky said that intersubjectivity provides the bridge between the known and the new. When we bridge the gap between the actual and possible, the performance and the potential levels, we move the child from the known to the new. Thus intersubjectivity provides the basis for communication and points to the possible extension of the child's understanding. You can make links with Rogoff's thoughts on guided participation where adults and children alongside one another in the everyday tasks of planting, cooking, weaving, selling or other work in the home or beyond are engaged in intersubjectivity. Here it is often the tasks themselves, intimately rooted in the needs and the lives of the people, that allow for meaning to be shared. Children have models to observe and words to listen to as they first watch and then participate in the life of their community. In this way they are drawn from the periphery into the centre, as full members of a community of practice. Do remember that you can create a community of learners in your setting.

RESPONDING TO WHAT YOU SEE AND HEAR

When you see a child do something unusual or say something interesting you respond to this with, perhaps, a smile or a positive comment like 'Well done!' This kind of feedback, whilst showing the child that you appreciate what she has done, is very general praise and gives her no clue as to what it is that you are pleased with. I am reminded of the story of a child new to the nursery class and being looked after by 4-year-old Nicola, who started to take her finished painting to show the teacher. 'Don't bother,' said cynical Nicola, 'She'll just say it is beautiful.' I quote this very often because it is so clear an illustration of how little effect empty praise has on learners. Feedback must be related to what the child has done or said and focused on one or more particular aspects to help the young learner know what it is that she has done well.

TRY YOUR HAND

Here are some vignettes. You should decide which adults gave helpful feedback or untargeted feedback. Say also what you might have said instead. They all come from a reception class.

- *The children have been given four pictures and have been asked to put them in the 'correct' order to match the story they have just heard. As the children work, the class teacher, working with one group, says to Mathilde, 'You are sitting so quietly and getting on with your work. Well done.'*
- *The teaching assistant, who is working with a different group on the same task, notices that Bruno has cut out the pictures very neatly but is having trouble putting them in order. She sits with him and says, 'What neat cutting out, Bruno. Can we sort these out together? Can you remember how the story started?'*
- *At the end of the session the teacher comments favourably on some of the work done by the children but singles out Roman for special attention. She says to the class, 'I was so pleased with what Roman did. He spent a long time looking at the pictures before he started cutting them out and then he arranged them in order on a piece of paper and could then tell me a really good story from the way he had organised the pictures. It wasn't the same story that I read you, but it was a very good story anyway.'*

How did you get on with this? It is clear that in the first example the child, Mathilde, was praised for being biddable and doing what she had been asked to do. Although this is a positive comment it does little or nothing to help Mathilde know what she has done well. All she has done is follow instructions. Bruno, in the second example, does get targeted feedback. He is praised for his physical skill of cutting and perhaps this is because he finds this difficult. But he is also given some suggestions about how to move on in this task by the questions the teaching assistant asks him. The feedback from the teacher in the plenary session focuses clearly on the intellectual demands of the task, and her feedback to Roman, who had not re-told the story in the sequence expected by the teacher, nonetheless focused on what he *had* done and not on what he had not done and gave him credit for his work and his thinking.

Specifically this teacher did several things to enhance learning:

- She mentioned how long Roman had stayed on task and in doing this she suggested to all the children that spending time doing something is worthwhile.
- She outlined the process he had gone through, scaffolding his learning by making him aware of the steps he took. Helping children develop their own awareness of their achievements is a crucial feature of good feedback.
- She managed to find what Roman produced worthwhile even though it had not met her original goal – for the children to put the pictures in the sequence of the story she had read to the them. In doing this she showed the child that there is often more than one way of solving the problem set.

THE PEDAGOGY OF LISTENING

This is a phrase used by the followers of Loris Malaguzzi and refers to the philosophy developed there relating to assessment and documentation. They see all human infants as being competent, curious and questioning and in their work with babies, toddlers and pre-school children they place an enormous emphasis on listening. Rinaldi (2006) says that listening is a metaphor for having the openness and sensitivity to both listening and being listened to so that we listen using all our senses. We might think of this as being sensitive to what is implied by the words, actions and silences of those we are paying attention to. She also says the listening must be considered as an active verb requiring making meaning and interpretation so that we hear the words or notice the actions but then have to make sense of what questions the child is asking, the theories she is forming and the support and help she needs. This is far from being easy to do and requires that we are prepared to be wrong, to change our minds, to recognise that listening is really the basis for learning.

Listening is accompanied by *reciprocal expectations*. When we speak we expect to be listened and responded to. For Rinaldi listening is an innate predisposition enabling the infant to experiment and explore and communicate.

There are implications in this for the competency of teachers and other practitioners working with young children. Malaguzzi said that a teacher is someone who can be the director or the set designer, the curtain or the backdrop, and sometimes the prompter. She also needs to be sometimes sweet and sometimes stern, perhaps the electrician, the giver of paint, the audience who sometimes is silent, sometimes applauds, always watches and is full of enthusiasm.

This is a little saccharine for my taste but there are things to be learned from this and I would suggest that, in your interactions with young children, you need to be aware of these things:

- take every child seriously and ensure that you let the child know that you do;
- pay attention to what the child says and does and try and interpret this in terms of what you know about the child;
- take notes or record in some way so that you can have a record to reflect on and keep;
- respond to the child if you infer that she needs help – materials, advice, encouragement, appreciation;
- ask questions related to what the child is doing to help the child know how to move on;
- give positive feedback that is targeted so that the child knows what you are focusing on;
- ensure that feedback covers all domains of learning – intellectual, physical, social, emotional, expressive, linguistic, personal;
- become a dialogic practitioner in the sense of setting up a real two-way dialogue with the learner;
- do not test the child or offer rewards.

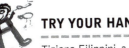

TRY YOUR HAND

Tiziana Filippini, a pedagogista (similar to an advisory teacher) in Reggio Emilia, has spent time thinking about the role of the adult and this is what she says:

*Sometimes the adult works right inside a group of children and sometimes works just around the group, so he has many roles. The role of the adult is above all one of listening, observing and understanding the strategy children use in a learning situation. The teacher has, for us, a role as dispenser of occasions; and it is very important for us that the child should feel the teacher to be, not the judge, but a resource to whom he can go when he needs to borrow a gesture, a word. According to Vygotsky, if the child has gone from point **a** to point **b** and is getting very close to **c**, sometimes to reach **c** he needs to borrow assistance from the adult at that very special moment. We feel that the teacher must be involved within the child's exploring procedure, if the teacher wants to understand how to be the organiser and provoker of occasions, on the one hand, and co-actor in discoveries, on the other. And our expectations of the child must be very flexible and varied. We must be able to be amazed and to enjoy, like the children often do. We must be able to catch the ball that the children throw us, and toss it back to them in a way that makes the children want to continue the game with us, developing, perhaps, other games as we go along.*

(Filippini 2009, cited in Edwards et al. 2012: 151)

English is not the first language for Filippini so you might find the language a little difficult to decode. But here are some things for you to think and try to work out.

- What do you think she means by the teacher being the dispenser of occasions? And do you think you are able to fill that role in your work? You certainly will if you are following children's interests and setting up activities or areas to reflect these.
- Which sentence summarises the ZPD and what is the role of the adult in that? The example given using letters of the alphabet is helpful in enabling the reader to think of the ZPD as something abstract rather than physical – a notional gap.
- Which of the examples below illustrates the metaphor of catching and throwing a ball?

45

1 *Halya builds a complex structure with blocks and is delighted that it does not collapse. She calls the adult over to admire her work. The teacher comments on the fact that it is symmetrical.*

2 *Abebech draws a picture of her little brother and when the adult sees it she says, 'Wow, he looks just like you! Same sparkling dark eyes. What will you do with it?' 'Give it to him,' replies Abebech, 'but he will just put it in his mouth.'*

3 *An adult tells all the children in assembly that Anna has done well and is a pleasure to have in class. When her mother hears about it she says, 'How lovely!' to which Anna replies, 'She says that every week about somebody.'*

The first two are clear examples of genuine sharing of attention and meaning, of intersubjectivity and of scaffolding. I hope this helps you to see the connections between interaction, attention sharing, scaffolding learning, expert others, guided participation and listening.

MOVING ON

In the next chapter we think about who the experts about individual children are and how we can tap into their sometimes privileged or specialist knowledge of the child.

Chapter 6

Who are the experts?

Rita Dunn, late professor at St John's University, New York – an expert on early childhood development – said: '*If the child is not learning the way you are teaching, then you must teach in the way the child learns.*'

TRY YOUR HAND

Who, would you say, knows the most about any individual child? This is a difficult question to answer and I would guess that many of you have said something like 'the class teacher' or 'the key worker'. You may also have said 'the parent(s)'. But what about the child herself? Read through the case studies below for examples of children communicating with others about what they know and can do.

- Khawar, described as being confident, articulate, not yet 5 years old, told her teacher who was struggling to communicate with a much younger child: 'She no . . . English . . . I can tell lots of Punjabi' (Dodwell in Marsh and Hallet 1999: 22).
- Victoria filled out an application for a pretend job in Pipe's Garage. In response to the question 'Why I would be good at the job' she said, 'I would be good because my daddy taught me to mend cars and so did my mummy. I'm good at using tools.' Adam, in the same class, chose to fill in a job application form to work at Pipe's Garage, saying 'I do it at my house' (Hall in Marsh and Hallet 1999: 116–17).
- Claire goes to school by bus. She knows that she is going the right way because she recognises some of the shops and the signs on the way. She knows that Daniel's the Hairdresser is where she has her hair cut; the letters 'BP' show her the petrol station where the car gets filled up and Sally's Sweet Shop is where she goes to spend her pocket money (Hallet in Marsh and Hallet 1999: 55, 57).

Khawar is clear about her linguistic abilities; Victoria and Adam are able to reflect on what it is that they can do which might enable them to play the roles they have chosen; Claire knows a great deal about her environment. These are four ordinary children. This may not be school knowledge but do you think that matters? Think about how important it is for all children to develop the specialist knowledge related to where they live, how they live, where they go to during the day, where their everyday lives take place.

We do sometimes have a tendency to dismiss young children as being not yet cognitively competent when often they are. Our views of children's competence may come from a very narrow and Western view of what competence is. Think about the things you may have read or seen of the lives of children in the developing world and reconsider. There is an example in the work of Rogoff (1990) where you can find a photograph of a baby of 11 months cutting a fruit with a machete. This appears to many here as shocking and dangerous and yet the reality is that, for many of the world's children, being part of the world of work is what life is about. The AIDS pandemic in sub-Saharan Africa left many young children as the heads of families. Street children in many African cities engage in complex transactions as they earn money to survive. This must make us think about how narrow our views of children, their competence and their capacities are. No one would want our children to have to deal with the difficulties these children have to deal with. But what we do need to think about is how we can consult children about their own feelings about what they are doing. We need to hear their voices and attend to what they say.

Gerison Lansdown (1996) reminds us that article 12 of the United Nations *Convention on the Rights of the Child* states that all children have the right to express their own views on anything that affects them and to have their views taken seriously. This applies not only to their family lives but also to anything that concerns their health, their education and their development. Educators have, traditionally, paid scant attention to this, particularly educators of young children. Often children are viewed as being in need of adult care and protection and advice, and it is clear that some children are, at times, certainly in need of these things. Evidence of the lives of children in less developed countries shows just how capable, competent and thoughtful young children have to be and how seriously they need to be taken.

In this country some schools and settings, taking the issue of children's rights seriously, have set up mechanisms for ensuring that children have some voice in the life of the school. This varies from very crude to relatively successful, where schools have school councils and peer mediators and mentors and so on. In some schools only children aged 7 and above are involved in these councils, while in others even children in the reception class are involved. Much depends on how these things are set up, but what children say about them is revealing.

TRY YOUR HAND

Read these case studies and analyse them in terms of children's sense of justice, right and wrong, fair and unfair. Look too for evidence of the child knowing how and where to find support.

The first of the case studies is one where the child has a very clear sense of injustice and also knows where to go for support.

Five-year-old Rowan said: 'I was smashed into the wall and I didn't do anything. I was just watching my friends and they were the ones being naughty. I was sent to Miss S's office and I had to stand there all afternoon and that was very unfair. I didn't tell Miss S who did it, but afterwards I went and found the peer mediator and told her and she told Miss S. And then I thought Miss S should say sorry to me but she didn't.'

(Personal communication)

Rowan's description of what happened is revealing. He explains the events but also makes a judgement about how he was treated, using the word 'unfair' which indicates a developing sense of justice. He didn't 'tell on' his friends, but found an extremely mature way of dealing with the situation by seeking out the peer mediator. His comment that the headteacher should have apologised to him, but didn't, shows how much he has internalised about what he is expected to do when he makes a mistake and how he generalises this to adults. He is learning something important about how rules for adults and children, or strong and weak, vary.

Contrast that with the second example relating to a child of similar age.

Four-year-old Amina came home very upset and told her mum she wasn't going back to nursery. It took a lot of gentle probing to find out what had happened but in the end Amina revealed the fact that two other little girls kept holding their noses when they sat next to her.

(Submitted by a colleague)

In this example Amina, thinking back over what had happened to her, recognised that something unfair had taken place. But it appears that there are either no structures for helping her deal with this in her nursery or she is not aware of them.

In terms of learning there are many excellent examples of classes or settings where provision is made for inviting children to assess their own achievements. In these, children are invited to reflect on their own learning. Young children are not dependent on adult evaluations and can make judgements about their own successes, and this is a crucial life skill.

EXPERT CHILDREN AND EXPERT ADULTS: LEARNING FROM NEW ZEALAND

You may recall reading about how early childhood workers in New Zealand create what they call *Learning Stories* for the children in their care. One of the most interesting things arising from this is how the children reveal their abilities to self-assess or reflect on what they can do and what they cannot yet do. It will not surprise you that it is the expert adults, working with the children, who plan for self-reflection and interact with the children in ways in which talking about yourself, as an equal partner, is fostered.

TRY YOUR HAND

This is an extract from an article called 'Young children reflecting on their learning: teachers' conversation strategies' written by Margaret Carr, whose work you encountered in an earlier chapter. As you read it think about what it is that the teacher K (Kim) does that enables the child, I (Isabella), to reflect on what she has done.

K: *So what did you practise?*

I: *A butterfly (points to the photos) and (pause) I did the red outside and then I did the blues and then the yellow (continues to point to the photos) and the purple and after that I let it dry, didn't I? (looks up at Kim)*

K: *(nods head) Mmm you did. (smiles)*

I: *A little bit and then I put that other tile (pointing to the photo), didn't I? (looks up at Kim)*

K: *(nods head) Yes, you did. (short pause)*

K: *And why did we let it dry?*

I: *Because it was a little bit sticked down (puts her fingertips together) wasn't it? (looks up at Kim)*

K: *(nods head) Mmm.*

I: *After the glue. And that's when we um let it dry out (pointing to photo) and then we put things on it, didn't we?*

K: *(nods) We did. We did.*

I: That's when I'm practising (pointing to photo) and that's when I did the tile things (pointing to more photos) and then after that we let it dry. (pause, looks at Kim)

K: Mmm.

I: (fingers moving) When we finished and then I let it dry (folds arms) and then we put that stuff on (joins hands together and wiggles fingers) on the top and then we let it dry after that didn't we? (big smile)

(Carr 2011: 257–70)

Did you notice that Kim managed to keep the conversation going by smiling, nodding her head and doing what Wood and Wood (1983) call *conversation oil* – the small and almost unconscious things we all do to keep conversations alive. She also affirmed many of the things Isabella has done through these actions and gestures. And she often used 'we' rather than 'I' or 'you' to help Isabella know that they are together in this process.

The article on which this is based is interesting and if you can find a copy do read it. You have been offered a very small taste of what Carr says and she moves on to thinking about not only what the adult does but also what children themselves do in terms of thinking about what they can do and why.

Here is how Carr summarises her findings:

She says that the value of children and educators *having conversations about learning* cannot be overestimated. At her university early childhood students are asked to use recording devices to record their conversations with children, analyse them and think about what they reveal. They show how often educators use closed questions – those requiring a yes or no or an 'only one possible correct answer' response. She found that children who are invited and expected to ask questions and have these listened to more easily become equal partners in any dialogue. Where children are able to follow an interest or a passion they are more likely to become very questioning and knowledgeable, opening up more possibilities for reflection.

PARENTS AS EXPERTS ON THEIR OWN CHILDREN

It is a truism that parents know their children better than anyone else and see their children in contexts which are not available to teachers or other practitioners. In order to fully appreciate what any individual child is interested in, able to do or struggles with it is important that their knowledge is recognised, valued and sought by practitioners. There will be parents who can tell you about the languages children speak, understand, read and/or write; the experiences children have had in their early years; the places they may have visited; the particular interests they have had and much more. But this should be a two way and equal exchange with practitioners able to discuss with parents or carers aspects of children's behaviour which might be difficult to understand and respond to. Here is an example:

> Two-year-old Imran irritates his mother by taking things from one place to another. He takes his clean clothes and puts them in the doll's pram, wheels them to his mum's bed, takes them out and puts them on the bed. Ten minutes later he wheels them back to his room and unpacks them. He transports things from one place to another.

You will have realised that this seemingly random behaviour is, in fact, recognised by educators as an important part of learning and development. Chris Athey (1991) pointed out that children – particularly between the ages of 2 and 5 – may engage in repeated patterns of behaviour in their attempts to draw on their previous experience in order to make sense of new experiences. As you know, Piaget called these repeated patterns *schemas*. Athey and others have described and defined a whole set of these schemas and you may recognise some of them. For example, the vertical schema is where a child is exploring the impact of up and down movements. You can see evidence of schemas in children's mark making and in their exploratory play. Other defined schemas include enveloping, rotation, going over and under, and so on. Practitioners aware of the importance of schemas in terms of learning can talk to parents so that they can both look out for them and recognise that they are not random and useless, but, on the contrary, essential to learning and development. But do remember that not all children engage in repeated patterns of behaviour. Doing so is not indicative of anything other than a particular interest. Not doing so means the child is using other means to follow up an interest.

PARTNERSHIPS WITH PARENTS AND CARERS: WHO KNOWS WHAT A GOOD PARENT IS?

It is important, of course, to set up close links with parents and carers and to ensure that there is a two way communication process in place. You may be the experts in terms of education but parents are experts in terms of their own children. Some parents will have different views and ideas from yours but do avoid the danger of assuming that there is only one way of being a 'good' parent and that is a very Western, white and middle-class way. Good parents are expected to attend open evenings, read with their children at home, support the setting or school in every way. The reality is that many parents are not able to do these things because of the pressures of their lives. Other parents may choose not to, thinking of teachers and educators as the experts and being unwilling to reveal what might be seen as their own inadequacies. So while parental partnerships may be desirable, it is important that educators are sensitive and aware of differences in expectations and experiences.

Research over many decades reveals that some fathers and many ethnic-minority parents may be very reluctant to attend parenting classes or to visit family centres. There is no doubt that many of these parents might indeed benefit from advice or support – as other parents may do – but something about the ways in which these classes or centres are set up is alien to them. Some interesting research from the USA described a programme called *Strengthening Families: Strengthening Communities* (Steele *et al.* 2000). Although this programme has much in common with other models of parental involvement it has some distinct and perhaps unique features. The most interesting is that it explicitly values the cultural history of the families and examines ways in which parents can be helped to pass this on to their children. This is a positive model and one that does not focus on problems.

In the first edition of this book the example of good practice in establishing and maintaining close professional contact between home and setting came from the *Thomas Coram Early Excellence Centre*, situated in a richly diverse community in central London. The example is retained because it is still in existence and still relevant. The focus of their partnership programme is the learning of the children. The partnership process involves operating a key worker system, having a long settling-in period, having in-depth conferences with parents about the child, ensuring that parents are kept informed about daily events, and organising regular times when parent and key worker can meet to review the child's progress. At these meetings the parent and key worker talk not only about the child's progress but also decide on priorities for the child's future learning and development and work out ways in which they can work together on this.

The staff at the centre recognise that parents are often working or studying and they continue to explore different ways of ensuring that all parents have access to information from the centre and a way of expressing their own views. These include the following:

- books which go from home to centre, in which key worker and parent record their views and thoughts;
- regular newsletters and information sheets;
- a website and use of technology where possible;
- invitations to parents to join particular projects;
- continually evaluating how effective the partnership is.

Some innovations have followed and been described by Valerie Wigfall (2002). They include trying to organise the setting and its surroundings into a *one-stop shop*. What this means is that it offers the following:

- an integrated network of agencies of services for children and families;
- a partnership between voluntary and statutory agencies into one body called *Coram Family*;
- coordinated inter-agency and cross sectoral working between professionals and services;
- open-access services for children and parents in the local community;
- outreach work for refugee and homeless families and those from particular ethnic groups – in particular the Bengali community;
- an attempt to coordinate provision to make it simpler for parents and carers to access and understand them (based on Wigfall 2002: 111–21).

EXPERT EXPERTS: OTHER PROFESSIONALS INVOLVED

Where you, or a parent, have serious concerns about some aspect of a child's development, you are able to seek the expert advice of a range of professionals. The experts involved may be asked to assess the children they see and communicate their findings to the school or setting. Such experts might include:

- *speech and language therapists*, who have a particular expertise in the acquisition and development of language;
- *educational psychologists*, who focus on the cognitive development of children;
- *clinical psychologists*, who focus on children's personal, social and emotional behaviour;

- *occupational therapists*, who can advise on particular aids for children with specific difficulties;
- *doctors, paediatricians, nurses and other health professionals*, who all have a role to play where there are questions about health;
- *social workers* and others involved when there are issues affecting the child and her family.

Your school or setting will be able to let you know which expert to turn to for problems you encounter. It is important for practitioners to establish professional relationships with these experts and to communicate as partners about the development of the child. You will recognise how important the specialist information any of these have about an individual child will be to your understanding of how the child is progressing.

MOVING ON

In the next chapter we think more carefully about what is currently known about the learning and development of children under the age of 3. You will appreciate that this is in preparation for knowing how best to monitor, understand, support and describe what they are doing.

Chapter 7

Babies and toddlers
Revealing their worlds

We must realise the enormous relevance of the insights coming from research on the under-3s for the whole of the educational system and how much potential there is for a bottom-up movement where early years takes the lead.

(Rayna and Laevers 2011: 169)

In the past few years there has been an enormous amount of research into the learning and development of the human infant from birth until the age of 3. One of the pioneers in researching early development was **Charlotte Bühler** who, as long ago as 1931, began to chart the social development of Austrian babies and toddlers as seen through their very early peer interactions. You may have encountered her work and also that of **John Bowlby** who talked of 'fear of strangers' as being a survival mechanism in human beings. This is where the human infant after first responding positively to all those encountered develops an awareness of a potential threat posed by having someone strange close by. He was influenced by the earlier work of Lorenz who paid attention to the imitative behaviour of young ducklings towards their mother. He called this imprinting and for Bowlby this illustrated how crucial attachments to the primary caregiver are. I am sure you all believe that establishing close and loving relationships is important but for Bowlby it was only attachments to the mother that were crucial for secure emotional development. Much doubt has been cast on this since it is clear that in many societies infants form attachments with fathers, with extended family members, with siblings and others.

This chapter looks at some of the most recent research into this area and is set out rather differently from previous chapters. It is based almost entirely on the papers from one journal which you will find cited later in the chapter.

WHAT WE LEARN FROM COLWYN TREVARTHEN

It is the work of Colwyn Trevarthen over decades that sets the tone for much of the current research. With his intent focus on the child in context, involved in interactions, sharing attention with others, able to show aesthetic preferences and much more he gives us – his readers – a very detailed and moving glimpse into the social, emotional, cultural and aesthetic worlds of the youngest learners. Many of you reading this book will be working or living with children under 3 and you may find surprising just how much your view of these children will change after reading some of the things that Trevarthen tells us. He does not make sweeping assertions but as a scientist his research has involved him in closely observing children in groups and contexts in order to find out why they are so keen, from birth, to share intentions, feelings and experiences with others. Much of his focus is on communication and he is eager that those involved with young children should learn to take into account the *perspective of the child*.

He tells us that children are *story-seeking* from birth. We often talk of the child as meaning-making and I wonder what you think the difference between story-seeking and meaning-making might be. For me, story-seeking means wanting not only to understand something but also to share it with others. So the child is intent on learning new ways of both expressing and sharing experience. This is a clear emphasis on the child as a full and equal participant in cultural, communicative exchanges in the home, the community, the creche or nido or setting. Trevarthen tells us that toddlers, when with other toddlers or older children or adults, want to discover how to use this body and mind that they have and so they engage energetically and confidently in learning by imitating and cooperating to build a shared culture. Where the group is composed of peers the culture created is a peer culture and it is dynamic, creative and richly responsive to the environment and wide open to learning with and from responsive adults. The key word for us in that last sentence is responsive.

We are used to thinking about babies and toddlers being in need of love and care. We sometimes think of them being in need of stimulation and models to imitate. More expert others are often the providers of tools – both physical and cultural – and rewards of smiles or words of praise. But

I wonder how many of you reading this have ever thought about the innate ability that the human infant has for making a positive contribution to society. And this is strange because Marion Whitehead – as long ago as 1978 – talked of the human infant having a 'zest for learning'.

So Trevarthen is telling us that when working with very young children we must offer more than care and protection but offer *opportunities for adventurous play in a rich environment*. And rich does not mean in terms of things that cost a lot of money but things that will offer challenges.

We must try and get inside the child's thinking so we are able to *identify and support the child's motives*. This means working out what it is the very young child is paying attention to, asking questions about, trying to express. So we need to consider how best to offer two-way communication which is essential for what Trevarthen calls *intent participation learning*. This is all complex stuff and if you are very interested in it I recommend you buy and read the *European Early Childhood Education Research Journal* 19:2 where you will find a set of interesting and relevant papers all related to the learning and development of the youngest children.

WHAT WE LEARN FROM ROSEMARY ROBERTS

You will probably not have heard of Rosemary Roberts and that is because she is a young researcher. She has been influenced by Trevarthen's work on interaction and also by the work of Bronfenbrenner, particularly his thinking on the concept of the *two person system*: the mother–child, father–child and father–mother dyads which are the basis of the child's very early world. She considers also the concept of *wellness* where the child's wellness and the wellness of her immediate family create what could be defined as normal well-being which would be synonymous with normal development. She coined the term '*companionable learning*' to refer to the intersubjectivity where the child and more expert other are engaged in an equal and reciprocal dialogue. And she invented the term *diagogy* to replace the one-sided term pedagogy. Diagogy is learning and teaching together. Roberts says that diagogy involves four aspects of wellness:

- physical well-being;
- communication in the sense of all interactions with the world;
- wellness in terms of belonging and boundaries; and
- agency.

In essence Roberts is saying that companionable learning will take place when there is an emotional content to what is being learned (in other words it is something that interests or concerns the child) and where the dyad is a secure one (perhaps mother and child). So development or learning is what flows from active engagement with the world and the people in it.

TRY YOUR HAND

Which of these two examples seems to you to fit the description of companionable learning?

Abi is 19 months old. She has just finished eating a bowl of ice cream and looks at her empty bowl and then, quizzically, at her mother and then at the open dishwasher. Her mother responds, 'No, not yet. All the things in there are clean. I have to empty it first. Put it there', pointing to the table.

(Loosely based on Roberts 2011)

Harry is 2 years old and goes to a playgroup twice a week. He is sitting at a table with two other children and one adult. On the table are some coloured pens and pieces of paper. He seems unsure of what to do. One of the other children takes a pen and starts to take the lid off it. The adult notices and says, 'No, not yet. You must wait for me to show you what we are doing.'

(Personal observation)

These are rather crude examples and it is easy to recognise that in the first example the child and her mother have an obviously close relationship and their communication involves gestures, words, and close looking. They are attuned to one another which enables them to communicate easily in a two way, reciprocal event associated with an everyday activity in the home. It could easily fit the definition of companionable learning. The second example, however, lacks the emotional link between the children and the adult and refers to a decontextualised task.

WHAT WE LEARN FROM THE WORK OF DION SOMMER, INGRID PRAMLING SAMUELSSON AND KARSTEN HUNDEIDE

The work cited here comes from some research published also in the *European Early Childhood Education Research Journal* but in a later edition than the examples discussed earlier. It focuses on the differences between child perspectives and children's perspectives. At first reading this might seem very trivial to you but read on.

- Child perspective(s) means that the attention of the adult is focused on understanding children's perceptions, experiences, utterances and actions in the world. This means that it is not the child's lived experience: it is always an adult approximation or interpretation.
- Children's perspective(s) represents children's own experiences, perceptions and understandings of their world – their lives. So the child herself is the subject of study.

You will perhaps have decided that this approach is close to that of both Trevarthen and Roberts. Those wanting to adopt a child perspective oriented approach in their practice will need to consider five basic assumptions, which are:

- *Seeing the child as a person* – one who has the same needs as other human beings. So the child will need to be seen, heard, respected, loved and influenced by others. This contrasts with the view in many settings where the young child, particularly the very young child, is seen as an object.
- *Empathetic participation with the child* – being able to enter into the child's world through careful listening and looking to grasp the meaning of what it is the child is uttering, doing, feeling.
- *An interpretative attitude of respecting the child's utterances and world of meaning making.* This requires seeing utterances as meaning ways of exploring, describing, experiencing and explaining. In essence the role of the adult is one of sensitive decoding.
- *Guiding the child in a sensitive way by adjusting and expanding what the child is doing.* This is very close to scaffolding or guided participation.
- *Recognising that early care and education must be a dialogical process where child and adult or more expert other are both teaching and learning – are equal partners in reciprocal actions.* The child and adult are co-producers of the education and care.

You will know that this is very often the way in which very young children learn within their homes where they, together with those who love them, come to make sense of features of everyday life. When very young children are spending their early years going to childcare there are two areas of socialisation for them, that of home and that of setting, and it is obvious to me – and will be to you – that the home and setting complement one another.

TRY YOUR HAND

Think about these statements and what they tell you.

Daniel Stern (1985: 4) said:

Since we can never crawl inside the infant's mind, it may seem pointless to imagine what an infant may experience. Yet that is in the heart of what we really want and need to know. . .These notions make up our working hypothesis about infancy.

Colwyn Trevarthen (1992) said:

Oh, listen to him! Yes! That's right. Tell me all about it – oh yes, you have so much you want to say.

Field (1990: 124) wrote:

In harmonious face-to-face interaction with infants, parents will reduce their tempo, exaggerate and repeat their movements, respond by imitating and enhancing their behaviour, turn-taking and respecting the infant's coincidental interruptions of the exchange. The infant appears attentive and contented.

Margaret Donaldson (in conversation with Colwyn Trevarthen) stated:

Human sense is the understanding of how to live in the human and physical worlds that children normally develop in the first few years of life. It is learned spontaneously in the course of the direct encounters with these worlds that arise daily and unavoidably everywhere, transcending cultural differences. It is universal except for children with very severe disabilities or extreme forms of deprivation that limit normal opportunities for interaction . . . The learning is continually informed and guided by emotion – that is, by feelings of significance, of value and of what matters. And it is highly stable and enduring, once established. It is the foundation on which all that follows must build.

(Cited in Trevarthen 2011: 179)

I have selected four really significant pieces – pieces that could influence your thinking and practice and so I recommend that you read each of these again, making some notes as you go. In each case ask yourself 'What am I learning from this?'

Here are the notes I made the first time I read each statement:

For me, the first one sums up what our philosophy should be based on – *getting into the mind of the learners.*

The second – which is a parent responding to the gurgling and vocalising of her baby – is a reminder of how *remarkable the human infant is in terms of making every possible effort to be part of her society, her culture and community and how the attentive parent or carer can respond to this.*

The third one is an evocative description of *how parents interact and what we can learn from this.*

And the last one is a wonderful summary of how important it is that the *things we offer to babies and toddlers should be rooted in real and significant things in their lives which mirror their interests or questions, the everyday world in which they live and responsive to feelings of being loved and cared for, listened to and respected.*

MOVING ON

In the next chapter we examine how some children in our schools and settings remain ignored or unheard for a range of reasons and consider what we should do to minimise and deal with this in order that we are planning for quality.

Chapter 8

Observing, planning and assessing for equity

It seems extraordinary to me that in the year 2015 there is still the urgent need to talk about how to support diversity in early years settings. Yet difference in terms of language, race, gender, class, culture, religion, ethnicity, economic circumstances and ability not only still exists but continues to create divides between groups rather than the respect and understanding so many have promoted. In this chapter we will examine the precocious competence of very young children in identifying difference and responding to it. We will identify which children are silenced or alienated and the effects this has on them as learners and as full members of the class or setting community. And we will ask the question: what can we do to create equity?

Let's start by asking you to perform a task.

TRY YOUR HAND

Make a list of the children with whom you work and notice which names come at the beginning of the list and those that come at the end of the list. Make a note of any you had quite forgotten. Now ask yourself why some were easy to remember and others less so. Here is what happened when a group of early childhood students I was working with did this same exercise.

Henry: Oh no! The first names are of all the children who put up their hands, do what I ask them and now I notice that all but one of them is white. And 7 of the first 10 are girls. And worst of all I completely lost five children and now I see that one is a boy with Down's Syndrome, two of them are speakers of Punjabi, one is a child who never says anything in class and another is a refugee child new to the group.

Alicia: I think my list is worse than yours. The first names are all boys, all the ones who are always in trouble. Then a whole group who I remember because they always sit together and talk a lot to one another – mainly girls. And I forgot five children who have English as a second language, two children who are late every day, a new boy who wears glasses and the little girl who never speaks.

Mariana: Perhaps because I am not a native English speaker I'm more aware of language as an issue and the first six names on my list are of children who are bilingual like me. The next six are girls – like me. Then there are a set of 12 names, all the children who are white and who sit together and are friends out of the setting. At the bottom of my list are the three children who come from the local flats which are always regarded as being very rough.

This is a crude piece of research but it is revealing in terms of how we all make assessments and judgements according to our own values and principles. I wonder what your list revealed to you about yourself and how you value the children in your care.

WHAT CHILDREN UNDER 3 KNOW ABOUT DIVERSITY

There is evidence from research in the developed world and increasingly in the developing world which shows that children, as they construct their own self, do so in terms of who is like them and who not. Oliveira-Formosinho (2001) showed that children at the age of about 2 notice differences like skin colour and gender. Derman-Sparks (1989) found that children of 18 months of age could classify their own photograph together with those of people of the same race. Glenda MacNaughton (2006) believed that children's identity in terms of gender is established by the age of 3. And they not only know what their gender is but also what clothes and toys and behaviours are related to that gender. So they understand that in some cultures and groups girls wear pink and boys wear blue, girls play with dolls and boys with guns, girls can cry but boys shouldn't and a great deal about what expectations the adults in their worlds have of them.

Yet it is evident that in many cultures there is still a certain blindness – called daltonism – in those caring for and teaching young children. They hold firm to a belief that young children are skin-colour blind, blind to social, economic and other differences. And professional programmes for educators and carers seem to do little to address this continuing belief.

Think about why this is important. Do you believe that you could talk easily and honestly to your colleagues about race and racism? Do you think that you relate in the same way to all the children in your groups – black, white, rich, poor, from single parent families or traditional nuclear families, or extended families, native speakers of English and those with little or no English? Do you see diversity as being a problem or an advantage? There is a body of research evidence which shows that attitudes of educationalists are still fixed in a white, middle-class way of seeing the world so that children from different backgrounds are still perceived as different in a negative sense rather than as bringing richness to the community of learners.

In 2001 the USA launched its laughingly named *No Child Left Behind Act* as its policy to ensure there were equal opportunities and access for all children. A wonderful title for a programme with laudable aims, and yet . . . it appears that this act is rooted in all the still-held beliefs that different means less-good, diversity equates with disability and the hierarchies of race, class and gender persist.

In a study based in Australia, Petriwskyj (2010) in a rather small-scale research project found that teachers in early years classes saw diversity as disability, learning difficulty or lack of English. Teachers were talking of school readiness and lack of funding. There was little awareness of the advantages to anyone of having difference in the class or setting.

So let us examine a study in Portugal which sets out to create a pedagogical perspective for early childhood education and teacher training that seeks to intervene in order to construct positive, respectful and adaptive attitudes to diversity.

PEDAGOGY-IN-PARTICIPATION

You may find this case study interesting. In Portugal, where there had been very little research into diversity, a particular programme was put in place with a strong focus on democracy and a commitment to take into account the needs of children both under and over the age of 3. Democracy is a key word here because equality means the right of every individual in any situation or setting to have equal access to what is on offer. That is what democracy means in theory: the reality often does not match that. But in Portugal the planners were determined to ensure that childhood institutions like schools and creches and training places for adults become democratic spaces that respect and honour diversity and empower all the actors. The planners of the programme were much influenced by the models offered in Reggio Emilia and also by the work of the great Brazilian educator, **Paulo Freire** who was primarily concerned with the education of illiterate adults but whose work pointed all educationalists to an awareness of the importance of ensuring that all participants in any venture are helped to become aware of what they need to know and do in order to transform or change a system. So the key features of the programme can be defined as follows:

- From birth, all environments need to ensure that the child is offered individual respect and a recognition of any perceived 'differences' in family structure, family position, in culture, religion, and nature.
- Children themselves learn about difference and celebrate diversity in terms of age, gender, ethnicity, language and more in a genuine and not tokenistic fashion.
- All adults involved with the children must respond to each child as an individual and support children's curiosity, attend to their questioning and interests and help them to find their own answers using as many means as possible.
- As in the provision in Reggio Emilia a culture of listening, of relationships and of respectful interactions is put in place and maintained, creating an environment where many things are discussed and explored and taken seriously.
- Children's learning is based in the daily real-life experiences in the very early years. As the children get older they encounter the tools and support to move towards more abstract learning.
- Systematic observations are made of the children to identify their interests and support them and to help children pay attention not only to their interests but to those of others around them.
- Children and adults engage in dialogue, each in turn being the teacher and the learner, the more expert and the less expert other.
- The role of parents is key and their voices and views are heard and attended to so that this dialogic model is more than dyadic and involves the child, the parent or carer and the educators.
- The training offered to new and existing practitioners includes a strong focus on awareness of diversity and consciousness in order to implement what they learn in the setting.

None of this is new but it is worth reminding ourselves of positive models and reinforcing the need to find diversity a positive rather than a negative challenge.

A CASE STUDY

I am quoting extracts from a piece called 'Supporting young children', written by Birgit Voss, a bilingual nursery class teacher in an inner London primary school first written 20 years ago in 1994 – and still highly relevant. It was included originally as one in a series of articles gathered together to form a course reader for students on an Early Childhood Education programme at the then University of North London. The original book was entitled *I Seed it and I Feeled it: Young Children Learning*. That book has since been republished first as *The Early Years: A Reader* and later as *Key Issues in Early Years Education*.

SUPPORTING YOUNG LEARNERS

So here we are, autumn 1994. A new term has begun and I have just finished the first week. What have we got in my class for the next four months? Who are these children that I am supposed to teach according to their needs and interests, taking into account the individual experience they bring to school? When I say 'I', of course, I don't mean 'I'. Actually, there are quite a few others involved in the 'delivery of the curriculum, providing a safe, happy and stimulating environment for all our pupils' (to quote Ofsted). There is Jean, the Nursery Nurse, and two Primary Helpers, who cover for our breaks. There is the lunchtime helper, our Section 11 teacher. (Unfortunately we only enjoy her company for one term. Next term she will take our transferring children up to the summer reception class which now starts after Christmas.) There is also my co-teacher who takes the class one day a week – I work four days per week. The head teacher comes to read a story once a week and we always have a number of students/visitors. Therefore 'I' am the leading member of quite a large team, which is trying to deliver our Early Years Curriculum. We all have different viewpoints, different strengths and values, different levels of awareness, different educational backgrounds (and different salaries!). Our teaching staff is entirely female, which most certainly has a limiting effect on some of our pupils, since we are able to offer no male role models. In 1982 in inner London there were twelve male nursery teachers out of a total of 600. We may express our aims differently. I might say, 'I try to ensure that each child has equal access to all areas of the curriculum. I know the forces and pressures of racism, sexism, class bias, able bodyism, ageism – and possibly other oppressive systems based on prejudice – might have a negative effect on our pupils' learning and well-being and may hold them back from fulfilling their whole potential.'

Jean, on hearing this, would probably look to the heavens and, with a sigh of exasperation, say, 'Oh, Be, what does that mean? Such jargon! How can our parents understand that? Can't we talk proper English with one another?' She has a point, of course, but Germans like me simply like to make long sentences! And the whole team would certainly agree that we all want our pupils to be happy.

So what have we got then, this term, and how can we ensure that they are all happily learning? For the first two weeks of term we have only the eighteen children who were part-time last term. Twelve stay for lunch, six go home and return afterwards. We have facilities to ensure a high quality lunchtime for twelve children only. Six children sit with a member of the team at each of the two tables and lunch is, of course, not simply about food intake. All areas of the curriculum can be covered in that one hour. It is often the right time for 'intimate' conversations and children have shared many family secrets, joys and pleasures and things that trouble them.

We already know these eighteen children quite well. Four girls and fourteen boys. Why do I get a slight sinking feeling looking at this distribution? Help! So many boys, such imbalance! Is this my sexism speaking? My fear of the many Batmans and Captain Scarlets trying to kill each other constantly, brandishing swords and pointing guns made from anything at all – sticklebricks, pencils, blocks, straws – noisy behaviour, looking so much more competitive and combative? Looking more closely I reassure myself that some of these fourteen boys actually don't like rough and tumble noisy play. It is more natural to them to do things quietly and gently. So there is some hope. And one of the girls has to be watched; she can be quite spiteful and vicious to others. Still, there is a better class dynamic when the boy/girl ratio is more even. It will get slightly better when our part-timers join us. Then we will have thirty-three children in all, more boys than girls, sixteen bilinguals (five at the beginning stages of English), one boy with speech problems, another with behaviour that borders on autism. I wonder if we should get the Educational Psychologist in to observe him?

Even though we know some of these children very well already, it is always surprising how one's expectations have to be adapted. Young children change at a fantastic rate and they often behave very differently when they start coming full-time. I consider it one of the beauties of our work: it's always full of surprises! The long summer holiday emphasises the changes. Some of our pupils have changed in appearance – different hair, grown taller, use words with greater sophistication, grown more confident. Some have become more attached to their parents and a previously happily settled boy is showing un-expected depths of rage, anger and upset at his mother's leaving. He is also using English now as though it was his first language (which is, in fact, Urdu). Yet another little girl who simply couldn't settle last term and whose piercing howls disrupted school life for weeks now smiles sweetly at her dad and with excited chatter in Bengali takes her leave from him. She takes Jean's hand, looks at her with big, trusting eyes, smiles again, gets a little cuddle and I am amazed once again. No tears at all? Yes, it's possible. Even the children we think we know very well we have to observe carefully again, make our mental notes about their progress and changes and, at the end of the day, when the last child has finally gone (usually picked up late), Jean and I swap our notes. At this stage we only record our observations verbally. Later on, when we have collected more data we will commit something to paper. Each child has a record where we enter relevant changes and collect samples of work.

This record is usually started at the home visit. It is an adapted version of the Primary Learning Record which is used by the other classes in our school . . . and parents help me to fill in the first page. It is our policy that each child gets this opportunity to meet me in the safety of her/his home environment. Last term, because of our continuous cuts in funding, the head teacher had to cover for my visits – an indication of how important we think this first home school link is. This term the Section 11 teacher will cover for my visits.

I usually take a puzzle, a book, some drawing material and a photo book with pictures of the team, the school, our class and the children at work. We look through this book together, often with grandparents, aunts and uncles, as well as parents and the child and siblings. I chat a bit about the kind of things children can do in our class. The pictures speak for themselves when I am unable to communicate in the family's language. That, and a great deal of body language, smiles, gestures usually get the message across.

During the visit, I also take some photographs of the child. They are used later when the child comes to school to mark her/his space on the coat hooks, the towel hook and the third, whole body one, for the magnet board. The home visit is a good opportunity to ask the parents to write their child's name in the family's language. I usually let them write it into the record. From there I can enlarge it on the photocopier at school and use it in our graphics area and anywhere else where the child's name appears in English. A very easy way to get dual language writing samples!

When these children join us (we admit one per session for about two weeks, starting during the third week of term) the often painful process of separation is facilitated by having met me and having talked about the visit with the parents. Naturally we do encourage parents to stay with their child as long as we think necessary.

From my home visits I know that some of the bilingual children joining us are very much at the beginning stages of learning English. I make a note of the different languages our little community will be using for the next four months: Gujarati, Bengali, Turkish, Urdu, Cantonese, Persian, Arabic, German and, of course, English. I check these against our present resources. We have cassette and video story tapes in all the languages but Cantonese. We have plenty of writing samples, newspapers and magazines in Chinese as we had some Chinese-speaking children earlier. When we celebrated Chinese New Year – the Year of the Dog – we stocked up during a visit to the local Chinese supermarket. We also have appropriate clothes, fabrics and home base equipment – and lots of pictures. The parents seemed very open, friendly and cooperative during the home visit. I am sure they would love to make some story tapes, maybe some songs for us – something to organise.

For the other bilingual children we probably, at this stage, do not need to prepare anything different from what we normally offer. The way children learn in our class is by firsthand experience, building on and extending what they already know, and this is ideally suited to acquiring another language. Children are encouraged to collaborate with each other and research has shown that bilingual children working and learning with their English-speaking peers get to know English very fast. We provide many opportunities for rehearsal and repetition of natural language patterns and, of course, we have many stories with additional visual support (things like story props, either two- or three-dimensional). The team is aware that often children in the beginning stages of learning English go through the 'silent period'. This is a time when data is collected and processed. They need to listen, observe and feel confident before they dare to utter the first English word. Bombarding them with direct questions, insisting on a response can be very intimidating during this time. How often do we teach by asking questions? Even I, who through my own experiences am very aware of this silent period phenomenon (I didn't dare speak an English word for nearly a whole year when I first came to this country!) catch myself asking silly questions, but having done so also provide the answer and do not expect it from the child. There are many opportunities in a busy nursery classroom in which spoken English is not a requirement for participation in an activity.

For example, there is the use of the magnet board. This is used for story props but also the photo cut-outs and names. The photo cut-outs consist of a full-length portrait of the child, cut out and covered in clear, self-adhesive film.

A bit of magnetic tape is stuck to the back which then sticks the picture onto anything metal. Often children, in groups or alone, arrange and re-arrange these figures, inventing their own stories or re-enacting familiar ones. They also get arranged according to friendship patterns. Occasionally one 'disappears' under the carpet or attempts are made to bite somebody's head off. I much prefer this aggression to be played out on the symbolic level than on the real person. A photo can be replaced!

The photo cut-outs have the potential to reflect the whole class community: big and small, staff and pupils, all have their miniature reflections there. Like the mirrors we also have in our classroom, they confirm immediately that everybody has their place in our class – everybody belongs. One's image is present, reflected and valued. This is part of our ethos. We try to represent in the classroom, through pictures, fabric, imaginative play materials, puzzles, dolls and books, all our children's and staff's different cultures. We have a number of small saris, Chinese jackets, chopsticks. We have photos of daddies changing nappies and bottle-feeding babies. There are pictures of women car mechanics, a woman 'milkman', Indian women washing their clothes in the river . . . There are pictures of African women carrying babies on their backs and water/food on their heads. We have photos of male and female fire fighters on the wall, etc. The most important resource is, however, the children and their work. They provide endless opportunities for extension and reflection. I use photography a great deal, despite the lack of money. School cannot pay for this expense any more, so now the cost is covered by the class fund – i.e. parental support. Each child has three places, as a rule, where their photo is displayed (as explained earlier). Additionally I have illustrated many daily routines and sequenced activities (e.g. We put out our toothbrush, go to the loo, wash our hands and sit down. This also has a little song). Things like finger painting, cooking, being outside, working in the garden, playing with water, looking after babies – anything at all can be extended further by making a little book, keeping it as a record. This is a valuable way of introducing literacy in a relevant, meaningful context.

The needs of bilingual children and beginner readers are similar, when it comes to book making. Both groups benefit from repetitive language patterns, easy and clear texts in different contexts with obvious clues to meaning. We have many, many photo books with very simple texts or captions. With some help from the parents these can easily become dual-text books.

A further check through my records on newcomers reveals another gap in our resources. A little boy will join us whose family consists of two mothers and a brother. We have nothing at all to reflect homosexual relationships in our class. How can I validate his experience? And will I break some sort of law if

I do so? Well, if I do then good teaching is probably illegal. And I do think that homophobia is one of 'the other oppressive systems based on prejudices which might have a negative influence on our pupils' learning and wellbeing and hold them back from fulfilling their whole potential'. Luckily I noticed that Letterbox Library have a book among their stock list which depicts a lesbian relationship. It's called *Asha's Mums* for £3.99. I am sure we can afford that and I will order it, although I do not know what it will be like. I do, however, trust Letterbox Library's judgement. Their books are carefully selected and screened. When this little boy and his mums come to our school they will find this book prominently displayed on the shelves and they can feel accepted and at home. I am looking forward to this term. It feels like it might be very stimulating and exciting. I just hope that I can stand the pace. Luckily we will be able to do a great deal more, thanks to the input of our Section 11 teacher. She has already made us a number frieze in Urdu, Bengali, Cantonese and English, using photographs of the children. And we are planning little outings with small groups and turn-taking games. We will be able to give more individual attention when listening to story tapes, and, having additional staff, we might try exciting recipes (maybe something Chinese or Indian) for our cooking session. We will be able to shop for the ingredients with the children beforehand – very good!

If we are even more lucky, perhaps the Turkish/Bengali mother-tongue teachers (appointed by our Education authority) will be allocated to our school and work with us for a few sessions. Grateful for little crumbs we have to be nowadays. In Sweden it is a child's statutory right to be taught in her/his mother tongue. Would that be too expensive? My guess is that it would cost half of what the Government has recently spent in all, introducing and changing the National Curriculum.

It is useful to learn a few words – maybe greetings – in all the languages of the children. We have these written up in the book corner and send the children home with a greeting in their home language. The Language Census of 1986 revealed that, in London schools, 172 different languages were spoken. That means that one quarter of all pupils have a home language other than English. The most frequently spoken language in 1987 was Bengali, followed by Turkish, Chinese, Gujarati, Urdu, Spanish, Punjabi, Arabic, Greek, French, Yoruba, Portuguese, Italian and Vietnamese. Under the Inner London Education authority this diversity was recognised and provision was made for it. For two years I worked for a team which specialised in making people working with young children aware of the needs of bilingual pupils. Many new resources were created by this team and we worked out a set of beliefs that guided our work . . .

Language issues must be tackled in the context of equality of opportunity and with particular reference to issues of race, gender and class. Bilingualism is a positive asset, an important resource that nursery staff should recognise, value and build on in the classroom.

It is essential for nursery staff to create an environment where children's diverse cultural experiences are recognised and shared in a positive way.

Parents have a vital role to play in their children's education both at home and at school. Their understanding of issues such as bilingualism, cultural diversity and racism can help to broaden the experience of everyone in the nursery. The learning of English as a second language can be supported by:

- bilingual children working and learning with their English-speaking peers;
- providing additional visual support;
- providing opportunities for rehearsal/repetition of natural language patterns;
- encouraging continued development of the home language;
- creating opportunities for informal interaction between adults and children and making maximum use of any opportunities that arise; and
- creating opportunities in which spoken English is not a requirement for participation in an activity.

Children should not be withdrawn from the usual nursery activities for ESL work as this can:

- deprive the children of a familiar supportive learning context where there are natural models of English; and
- create divisions and resentment between children and pass on negative messages about the place of bilingualism in this society.

The cognitive development and linguistic development of children are closely linked and this needs to be considered when organising resources and activities both in children's home language(s) and in English.

(Finkelstein, L., 1990, *Primary Teaching Studies*, vol. 5, no. 2, February 1990)

The kind of teaching that benefits bilingual children is good teaching which will benefit all children.

TRY YOUR HAND

Re-read that and decide what you have learned from reading it about how to become a practitioner really committed to working for a culture of respect, democracy, listening and appreciating what diversity brings with it. Birgit's words have remained in my head for 20 years and it saddens me deeply to think that we seem to have made so little – if any – progress in this field.

Chapter 9

Assessing your offer
Quality learning

I am starting this chapter by quoting almost all of a chapter written by Mary Jane Drummond who analyses just what you get from observing the children and what the children get from being observed. I offer this as the introduction to thinking about how to examine and consider everything you offer in order to identify what it is that you do that makes your place of learning one of quality.

Drummond asks first:

Watching children: What's in it for us?

All adults who spend time with young children inevitably spend much of that time just watching them. We do so, in part, in the interests of their physical safety . . . But there's more to watching children than this.

First and foremost, when we watch young children, we can see them learning. And young children's learning is so rich, fascinating, varied, surprising, enthusiastic and energetic, that to see it taking place before one's very eyes, every day of the week, is one of the great rewards of being with young children, as educator, carer or parent. In a sense, watching children is its own justification. It opens our eyes to the astonishing capacity of young children to learn. . . But when we watch children we do more than simply marvel at their intellectual and emotional energy; we can also learn, by watching carefully and thinking things over, to understand what we see.

Our own observations can help us understand what the great pioneers of early childhood care and education have taught us about children's learning. Our own observations can illuminate the work of psychologists, researchers and educators. As we watch and listen, their work seems less remote, academic or theoretical: the children bring it to life. As we listen to young children talking, for example, we can understand more clearly the work of Gordon Wells who wrote about how young children work hard, day after day, at 'making meaning', slowly piecing together their understanding of the puzzling people and things and ideas that make up the exciting world around them. He used expensive radio microphones, a large sample of children and a sizeable research team to collect his data; but we can learn about children's talk, about children making meaning, in a more straight-forward way, simply by watching and listening attentively. And we can learn for ourselves what Chris Athey (1991) calls children's 'schematic behaviour', and about what Margaret Donaldson (1978) calls 'disem-bedded thinking', and about what John Matthews (1994) calls children's 'early mark-making' – we can learn all this, and more, simply by observing children.

Drummond here reminds us that, in order to make yours an offer of quality you need to know something about what is thought about how children develop and learn. You can do this by reading, by going to hear others talk, by running workshops for your peers and colleagues – and I hope, by reading this book. Staying aware is crucial.

DRUMMOND'S LITTLE CASE STUDY: AN AUTUMN STORY TO SET THE SCENE

One day I was talking to a teacher who seemed to be very agitated and frustrated. She told me about a boy of five she was working with, on a part-time basis, giving individual support in the classroom, because the educational psychologist had diagnosed him as having special learning difficulties. That diagnosis may or may not have been accurate – but the teacher was certainly having teaching difficulties, and, understandably perhaps, she was blaming the child. 'He's so ignorant,' she told me, 'so deprived and inexperienced. He doesn't know anything.' Thinking this unlikely, I asked her to explain a little – what was the evidence for these alarming charges? 'I'll give you an example,' she said. 'He doesn't even know what a conker is!' Since this conversation took place in October, when all over the country children's pockets were full of conkers, I found this story hard to believe and I wanted to know how she knew her pupil didn't know what a conker was. The teacher explained she had shown the boy a conker and asked him what it was. He replied: 'It's an acorn.'

Now, with some genuine, first-hand evidence in front of us, we can start to interpret and judge for ourselves. Do you agree with the teacher's verdict? Ignorant? Deprived? Inexperienced? Or do you see something else? Do you see an active learner, an interested enquirer, a meaning-maker? Do you see a child who recognises the object the teacher shows him as the autumnal fruit of a deciduous tree, but who has, in a moment of inattention perhaps, given it the wrong lexical label? Just as we sometimes, inadvertently, say right when we mean left (a mistake which can make quite a difference to a car driver in a busy city centre!).

To say 'acorn', when your teacher expects you to say conker, is evidence, as I see it, of both knowledge and experience, combined (unluckily for the child) with nothing more serious than a momentary lapse of memory. Had the child answered at random, uttering words from a totally different area of his experience ('lollipop', say, or 'fire-engine'...), we might have cause for concern. But he didn't. In his search for the name of the object being shown to him, he went, so to speak, to the correct filing cabinet in his mind, opened the right drawer, pulled out the appropriate file – but handed his teacher the wrong sheet of paper.

We are reminded here of the importance of trying to focus on what any child *can do and does know* instead of on the negatives of what the child does not yet know and cannot yet do.

Drummond now asks:

Observing children: What's in it for them?

We have seen how observing children, if we do it carefully, attentively, thoughtfully, generously, can give us insights into the richness of their learning. There are other important reasons for observing, trying to make sense of what we see: these are to do with the responsibilities of the adults who care for and educate young children. *Young children's awesome capacity for learning imposes a massive responsibility on early years educators to support, enrich and extend that learning.* Everything we know about children's learning imposes on us an obligation to do whatever we can to foster and develop it: the extent to which we succeed in providing environments in which young children's learning can flourish. We cannot know if the environments we set up and the activities we provide for young children are doing what they should, unless we watch carefully, to keep track of the learning as and when it takes place.

Observing learning, *getting close to children's minds and children's feelings, is part of our daily work in striving for quality.* What we see, when we look closely, helps us to shape the present, the daily experiences of young children in all forms of early years provision. The act of *observation is central to the continuous process of evaluation, as we look at what we provide and ask: is it good enough?*

Our careful observation of children's learning can help us make this provision better. We can use what we see to identify the strengths and weaknesses, gaps and inconsistencies, in what we provide. We can use our observations to *move closer to quality provision for all children, and for individuals.* We can *identify significant moments in a child's learning, and we can build on what we see.* If you had observed the child with the shell [cited earlier in this book on page 13], how would you take her learning further? What would you bring in for her to explore? A stethoscope? A hearing trumpet? A megaphone? Or other kinds of magnifiers – binoculars or a telescope? You might invite her to use her fingers to shrink and enlarge images on a tablet. Perhaps you would invite her to experiment with the enlarging button on the photocopier; or she might be intrigued by the images of shells thrown on a wall by an overhead projector – she would soon discover how to control the size of the image. Your observation would have helped you to help her – to take her one step further in her exploration of the world and how it works.

And the boy with the conker? What's the next step for him? Further observation, I think, and, preferably out of doors to start with, closer to oaks and chestnuts – and ash trees, sycamores, spindle bushes, sweet chestnuts and privet hedges. Back indoors, he may be intrigued by what's inside these fruits of the hedgerows. You can find out what interests him by watching, trying to understand what he is trying to understand. You can look back, to see what he has already learned; and then look ahead, and see the learning that is just about to take place, in the immediate future. With this understanding, you can be ready to support him and his learning: you can recognise his past achievements.

It is through watching and analysing we can start to *support and extend learning.* Only by noticing what it is the child is paying attention to, interested in, asking questions about can we start our job of scaffolding learning and enabling the learner to move from being able to do something with help to being able to do it alone.

Drummond suggests that through observation *we get closer to children's learning, thinking, questions — their pressing intellectual and emotional concerns.*

There is a wonderful example of an educator doing just this in Tina Bruce's book, *Time for Play* (1991). A teacher notices an excited group of four-year-olds causing chaos just outside the home-corner. The noise level is unacceptably high; all the dressing up clothes are on the floor, and the children are crawling under them, over them and through them. At a moment like this, does a teacher trust children's intellectual strengths? Or call for a return to order? Can an adult believe that children are searching for meaning and understanding, when the careful order of the classroom environment has been so violently disrupted? This teacher did. In a sudden rush of faith and confidence, remembering the 'Peter Rabbit' story she had read them the day before, she realises they are burrowing. When the children confirm her insight, she finds some old sheets, bedspreads and four old clothes' horses, and, with her support, the children soon make a wonderful burrow. They are not in dreadful trouble for infringing classroom regulations: they are free to continue their imaginative play, based on the enclosing/enveloping schema that is the present centre of their interest.

A friend of mine, an infant teacher, whose classroom is a place of genuine intellectual search and discovery, talks about watching out for 'the grain of children's thinking'. All too often she says, teachers teach across the grain, failing to recognise the children's concerns, pressing on with their lesson plans, their aims and objectives, or the next section of their topic webs. All too rarely, she argues, do educators take the time to observe, time that will be well spent if it shows them the way that children are going; *educators who get close to children's thinking in this way will be well placed to cherish and nourish that thinking.* Getting close to learning, then, is a worthwhile goal for every educator; but getting close, we must never forget, does not mean taking over. If we set about doing children's thinking for them, pointing out their errors and misjudgements, showing them the proper way to do things, and telling them all the right answers to the problems they set themselves, there will be precious little left for them to do.

For example, a group of young children spent twenty-five minutes absorbed in water play. The nursery nurse had, at their request, added some blue dye to the water, and the children were intrigued by the different shades of blue they could see: paler at the shallow margin and darker at the deepest, central part of the watertray. One child was even more interested in another, related phenomenon. He spent nearly ten minutes of this period of water play observing his own shoes and how their colour appeared to change when he looked at them, through the water and the transparent water-tray. The child seemed to be fascinated by what happened when he placed his feet in different positions; he leaned intently over the tray to see what colour his shoes appeared to be at each stage. He did not, of course, use the words 'experiment' or 'observation', but that was what he was engaged in, none the less. After each trial, he withdrew his feet into the natural light of day, as if to check that they retained their proper colour. Had the dye stayed in the water, where he'd seen it put? Or had some of it seeped out, into his shoes?

At the end of the morning session, the teacher and nursery nurse announced that it was time to tidy up. The children worked together to empty the water-tray of the sieves, funnels and beakers they had been using. They took out the jugs, the teaspoons and the ladles, emptied them and put them away. When they had nearly finished, the boy stopped and asked aloud of no-one in particular, 'How do we get the blue out?'

There is, of course, more than one way that an educator could respond to this question. But the one way that will do nothing for the child's learning, or for his understanding, is to tell him that it can't be done, or that he is wrong to even speculate about the possibility. The 'grain' of this child's thinking was running another way. Now the educator's task is not to take over, redirect his thinking, or solve his problem for him. The respectful educator, who is close to his chain of thought (following the grain of his thinking) will, rather, help him plan his next experiments, and the observations that will, finally, satisfy him, that not all changes in colour are reversible (shoes, yes, sometimes; water, sometimes, no).

The advice here is to *notice the grain of thinking* – the essence of what it is that the child is paying attention to – and go with it and not against it. Plan activities in response to what you notice one or more children are paying attention to, observe what happens, then extend or change or abandon the activity.

Here is Drummond's *end piece.*

Glenda Bissex is an American author and educator who, while studying for her master's degree in education, was trying to read one afternoon when her five-year-old son Paul wanted to play with her. Frustrated in his attempts to make her put down her book, Paul disappeared for a few minutes. When he returned, it was with a piece of paper on which he had printed, with rubber stamps from his printing set, the letters R U D F (Are you deaf?). His mother was dumbstruck and, in her own words: 'Of course, I put down my book' (Bissex 1980: 3). From that moment on she added to her academic study of the early acquisition of literacy the daily practice of observing her own son learning to read and write. Her account of what she saw is fascinating reading – not just for its entertaining title 'GNYS AT WRK' (taken from a note Paul pinned on his bedroom door at the age of five-and-a-half) – but also because of the way she uses her own, personal, first-hand observations, of her own first-born child, to throw light on young children's learning in general.

But she also takes every opportunity to raise difficult and challenging questions about the relationship between teaching and learning. There are passages in her book which make uncomfortable reading for all of us involved with young children's learning; Bissex suggests, gently, but firmly, that all too often children learn in spite of our attempts to educate. She emphasises, as I have tried to do throughout this chapter, the vital importance of listening, watching and waiting, if we are to have any hope of supporting and extending children's learning. In her unforgettable words:

> We speak of starting with a child 'where he is', which in one sense is not to assert an educational desideratum but an inescapable fact: there is no other place the child can start from. There are only other places the teacher can start from.
>
> (Bissex 1980: 111)

Observing children is simply the very best way there is of knowing where they are, where they have been and where they will go next.

(Adapted from Drummond 1998,
in Smidt (ed.) 2010)

BECOMING AN ACUTE AND ANALYTICAL OBSERVER

This book is about observation and assessment and its role in the learning and development of young children. One of the best ways of becoming an acute and perceptive observer is to try and evaluate what you offer the children – and their parents and carers. There are many facets of your provision to consider. Here, in outline, are some of the things you will be examining.

You will want to critically examine the *resources* you are able to provide and the *activities or projects* you offer. With regard to this the questions you should be asking might include the following:

- Does this reflect the observed interest of any of the children?
- Are the children using this equipment or not?
- What should I change and why?
- How could I extend the opportunities for learning in what I have set up?
- Does what I have put out reflect the cultures and the languages of the children?

You will want to consider the *interactions* you and the other adults have with the children and here you may be asking questions like these:

- Is the learner/learners competent in this situation?
- Are the children asking questions?
- Are the children interested/paying attention?
- Are the children interacting with other children?
- Are the children interacting with adults?
- Are the adults listening to the children?
- Are the adults interpreting what they see?
- Are the adults interacting with one another?
- Is there evidence of shared attention or intersubjectivity?
- Are the relationships reciprocal and respectful?

You will want to examine how you and your colleagues *communicate with parents and carers*. Here are some questions you might ask:

- Do you and your colleagues know the names of the children?
- Do you and your colleagues always greet the children and their parents/carers?

- Do you have regular times to meet?
- Do you listen to parents as well as tell them things?
- Do you have access to translators and interpreters?
- Do you send information home and how accessible is that to the parents and carers?
- Do you share your observations with parents on a regular basis?
- How do you do this?

You cannot claim that you offer a quality learning environment unless you document children's learning and do this in a way which is fair and transparent and available to the children themselves, to your colleagues and to the parents and carers.

- Are you documenting individual progress using a range of tools – photographs, displayed work, videos, learning stories, annotated examples?
- Do parents feel that they are listened to? How do you know?
- How effectively do you document the progress of each individual child?
- How do you make it possible for parents to have a record of significant moments in the lives of their children?
- How do you make evident that the languages and cultures of all the children are respected and reflected?

I recognise that this is a rather overwhelming list of questions. They are here to help you develop your own ability to raise questions which is what you must do if you are to be able to analyse and improve your offer. You are, wherever you are, whatever children you are working with, in a position to qualitatively change their learning and their lives. I hope you will come to feel just what a privilege that is!

Bibliography

Athey, C. (1991) *Extending Thought in Young Children: A Parent–Teacher Partnership.* London, Thousand Oaks, New Delhi, Singapore: Sage/Paul Chapman

Axline, V. (1964) *Dibs in Search of Self.* New York: Ballatine Books

Bissex, G. (1980) *Gnys at Wrk: A Child Learns to Write and Read.* Cambridge, MA: Harvard University Press

Bruce, T. (1991) *Time for Play in Early Childhood.* Abingdon: Hodder Education

Carr, M. (2001) *Assessment in Early Childhood Settings: Learning Stories.* London, Thousand Oaks, New Delhi, Singapore: Sage

Carr, M. (2011) 'Young children reflecting on their learning: teachers' conversation strategies', *Early Years: An International Research Journal* 31:3, 257–70

Carr, M. and Lee, W. (2012) *Learning Stories: Constructing Learner Identities in Early Education.* London, Thousand Oaks, California, New Delhi, Singapore: Sage

Derman-Sparks, L. (1989) *Anti-bias Curriculum: Tools for Empowering Children.* National Association for the Education of Young Children. Issue 242 of NAEYC Series

Derman-Sparks, L. and Ramsey, P. (2006) *What if All the Kids Are White? Anti-bias Multicultural Education with Young Children and Families.* New York: Teachers College Press

Dodwell, E. (1999) '"I can tell lots of Punjabi": developing language and literacy with bilingual children', in J. Marsh and E. Hallet (eds), *Desirable Literacies: Approaches to Language and Literacy in the Early Years.* London: Chapman

Donaldson, M. (1978) *Children's Minds.* London: HarperCollins

Donaldson, M. in conversation with Trevarthen, C. (2011) 'What young children give to their learning, making education work to sustain a community and its culture', *European Early Childhood Research Journal* 19:2, 173–93

Drummond, M. (1998) 'Observing children', in S. Smidt (ed.), *The Early Years: A Reader* and (2010), *Key Issues in Early Years Education,* 2nd edn of *The Early Years: A Reader.* London and New York: Routledge

Field, T. (1990) *Infancy.* Cambridge, MA: Harvard University Press

Filippini, T. (2009) cited in C. Edwards *et al.* (2012), *The Hundred Languages of Children,* 3rd edn. Santa Barbara, Denver, Oxford: Praeger, 151

Forman, G. (2012) 'The use of digital media in Reggio Emilia', in C. Edwards *et al.* (2012), *The Hundred Languages of Children,* 3rd edn. Santa Barbara, Denver, Oxford: Praeger, 348–55

Forman, G. and Fyfe, B. (2012) 'Negotiated learning through design, documentation and discourse in Reggio Emilia', in C. Edwards *et al.* (2012), *The Hundred Languages of Children,* 3rd edn. Santa Barbara, Denver, Oxford: Praeger, 247–72

Geertz, C. (1973) *The Interpretation of Cultures: Selected Essays.* New York: Basic Books

Hall, N. (1999) 'Young children, play and literacy: engagement in realistic uses of literacy', in J. Marsh and E. Hallet (eds), *Desirable Literacies: Approaches to Language and Literacy in the Early Years.* London: Chapman

Hallet, E. (1999) 'Signs and symbols: environmental print', in J. Marsh and E. Hallet (eds), *Desirable Literacies: Approaches to Language and Literacy in the Early Years.* London: Chapman

Halpenny, A.M. and Pettersen, J. (2014) *Introducing Piaget: A Guide for Practitioners and Students in Early Years Education.* London and New York: Routledge

Isaacs, S. (reprint 1999) *Intellectual Growth in Young Children.* London and New York: Routledge

Lansdown, G. (1996) *A Model for Action from the Children's Rights Development Unit: Promoting the Convention on the Rights of the Child in the United Kingdom.* Florence: UNICEF

Lansdown, G. (2005) *The Evolving Capacities of the Child.* New York: United Nations Publications

MacNaughton, G. (2006) *Shaping Early Childhood: Learners, Curriculum and Contexts.* Maidenhead: Open University Press

Matthews, J. (1994) *Helping Children to Draw and Paint in Early Childhood: Children and Visual Representation.* London: Hodder and Stoughton

Nash, M. (1967) 'Machine age Maya', in B. Rogoff (1990), *Apprenticeship in Thinking: Cognitive Development in Social Context.* New York and Oxford: Oxford University Press

Oliveira-Formosinho, J. (2001) 'The specific professional nature of early years education and styles of adult/child interaction', *European Early Education Research Journal* 9, 57–72

Oliveira-Formosinho, J. and Barros Araujo, S. (2011) 'Early education for diversity: starting from birth', *European Early Childhood Education Research Journal* 19:2, 223–35

Pahl, K. (1999) *Transformations: Children's Meaning Making in a Nursery.* Stoke-on-Trent: Trentham Books

Paley, V.G. (1929) *Bad Guys Don't Have Birthdays.* Chicago and London: University of Chicago Press

Paley, V.G. (1981) *Wally's Stories.* Cambridge, MA, and London: Harvard University Press

Petriwskyj, A. (2010) 'Diversity and inclusion in the early years', *International Journal of Inclusive Education* 14:2, 195–212

Rayna, S. and Laevers, F. (2011) 'Understanding children from 0 to 3 years of age and its implications for education. What's new on the babies' side? Origins and evolutions', *European Early Childhood Research Journal* 19:2, 161–72

Rinaldi, C. (2006) *In Dialogue with Reggio Emilia: Listening, Researching and Learning.* London and New York: Routledge

Roberts, R. (2011) 'Companionable learning: a mechanism for holistic well-being development for babies', *European Early Childhood Research Journal* 19:2, 195–205

Rogoff, B. (1990) *Apprenticeship in Thinking: Cognitive Development in Social Context.* New York and Oxford: Oxford University Press

Siraj-Blatchford, I., Sylva, K., Muttock, S., Gilden, R. and Bell, D. (2002) *Researching Effective Pedagogy in the Early Years project and Effective Provision for Pre-School Education*

Smidt, S. (2008) *Introducing Vygotsky: A Guide for Practitioners and Students in Early Years Education.* London and New York: Routledge

Smidt, S. (2011) *Introducing Bruner: A Guide for Practitioners and Students in Early Years Education.* London and New York: Routledge

Smidt, S. (2012) *Introducing Malaguzzi: Exploring the Life and Work of Reggio Emilia's Founding Father.* London and New York: Routledge

Smith, M. (2010) 'Let's make honey', in S. Smidt (ed.), *Key Issues in Early Years Education.* London and New York: Routledge

Sommer, D., Pramling Samuelsson, I. and Hundeide, K. (2013) 'Early childhood care and education: a child perspective paradigm', *European Early Childhood Education Research Journal* 21:4, 459–75

Steele, M. *et al.* (2000) *Strengthening Families: Strengthening Communities: An Inclusive Parent Project.* London: Racial Equality Unit

Stern, D. (1985) *The Interpersonal World of the Infant: A View from Psychoanalysis and Development Psychology.* London: Karnac Books

Trevarthen, C. (2011) 'What young children give to their learning, making education work to sustain a community and its culture', *European Early Childhood Education Research Journal* 19:2, 173–93

Twardosz, S. (2012) 'Effects of experience on the brain: the role of neuroscience in early childhood development and education', *Early Education and Development* 23:1, 96–119

Voss, B. (2010) 'Supporting young children', in S. Smidt (ed.), *Key Issues in Early Years Education.* London and New York: Routledge

Vygotsky, L.S. (1977) 'Play and its role in the mental development of the child' (C. Mulholland, trans.), in M. Cole (ed.), *Soviet Developmental Psychology.* White Plains, NY: M.E. Sharpe, 76–99. (Original work published 1933/1966.)

Vygotsky, L.S. (1978) *Mind in Society.* Cambridge, MA: Harvard University Press

Vygotsky, L.S. (1987) *The Collected Works of L.S. Vygotsky*, vol. 1. New York: Plenum

Wigfall, V. (2002) '"One-stop shopping": Meeting diverse family needs in the inner city', *European Early Childhood Education Research Journal* 10:1, 111–21

Wood, D. and Wood, H. (1983) 'Questioning the pre-school child', *Educational Review* 35:2, 149–62

WEBSITES

Charles Darwin, http://www.darwinproject.ac.uk/observations-on-children, accessed 31 December 2014

http://www.foundationyears.org.uk/files/2012/03/A-Know-How-Guide.pdf, accessed 31 December 2014

http://www.theguardian.com/theguardian, accessed 31 December 2014

Index

Entries in **bold** indicate chapter titles.